THE ULTIMATE GUIDE

TO

DOMINO TOPPLING

Over 160 Tips and Tricks to Becoming a Domino Toppling Master

The Ultimate Guide To Domino Toppling

our story

We started Bulk Dominoes with a mission: make the highest quality stacking and toppling dominoes and offer them to the world in bulk. Growing up, we only had small domino sets and dreamed what we could build if we had buckets and buckets of them. This vision became Bulk Dominoes. Now, making more dominoes than we had ever imagined, people all over the world are able to build massive domino setups, right in their own homes with the greatest dominoes we never had. We didn't stop at just making dominoes though, we have developed specialty parts and accessories to complement the building and stacking experience to make the domino toppling world more fun than ever before.

Building and designing with dominoes are great for STEAM learning - Science, Technology, Engineering, Arts, and Mathematics. Stacking and toppling dominoes builds skill, patience, and an immense level of accomplishment and satisfaction. Bulk Dominoes is proud to develop and support STEAM centered products and activities, now and into the future.

Bulk Dominoes' products are used and trusted by the industries top artists in the making of movies, commercials, world records, videos, and large promotional and entertaining activities. We are proud to deliver the same high quality dominoes on each and every order that ships from our factory. We maintain a strict quality control program that governs every piece and product that we manufacture. We are truly honored and grateful knowing people of all ages, from all corners of the world, use our dominoes to bring people together and have fun.

All of our products are proudly made in the USA.

STACK 'EM HIGH, LET 'EM FLY!

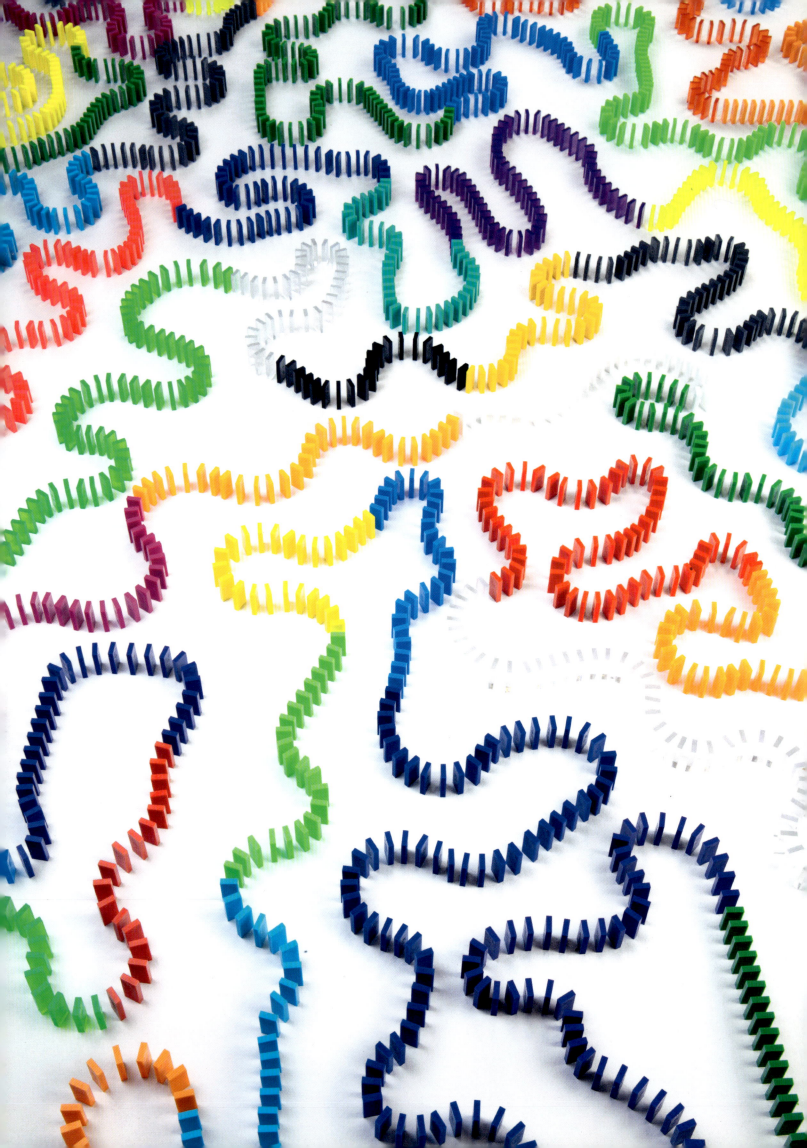

Acknowledgments

This book is a collection of tips and tricks from us and a community of wonderful topplers and artists. Topplers from all around the world have dedicated countless hours to the development and advancement of stacking and toppling dominoes with incredible tricks and techniques. We acknowledge and respect all of their great contributions to the world of domino toppling. The domino world would not be as fun, interesting, lively, and exciting without all those who have participated in building dominoes from the beginning to now.

Only a few ever reach the heights of true mastery. For those that do, we applaud, cheer, and enthusiastically encourage them! They are known for their breathless skill, major accomplishments, strategic stacking, intelligent designs, and snappy dynamic setups. It's amazing to see the creativity and the geniusness that allows them to do so much with one little block. The collaborations, the group activities, and the spreading of the knowledge of how to do domino toppling is one of the things that makes this activity so fun in the community.

This book does not represent all that is possible in domino toppling and building. There are many great and fascinating things discovered all the time by creative minds. Thus, this book was designed to be a companion and help for all those interested in getting into this great domino toppling experience. We look forward to all the intricate thoughtful structures, the unbelievable patience and perseverance in building those tough setups. It's this dedication and mental stamina that spurs thought into matter, weaves simple ideas into complicated working solutions, and grants the much needed life into the thought resolution process.

More than anything else, this book is about sharing the joy and delight of domino building and toppling fun. Rise to the challenge. Build on those that have come before. Perfect the world of domino toppling and share the love and enjoyment of these fun little blocks we call dominoes.

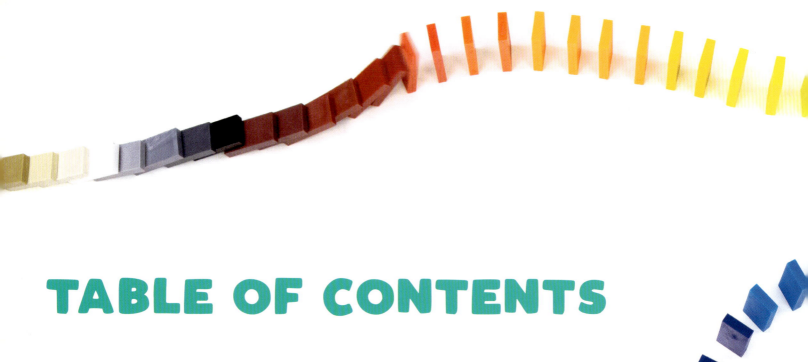

TABLE OF CONTENTS

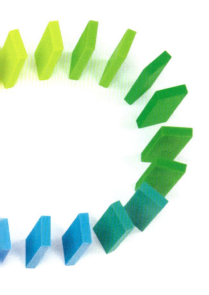

8	INTRODUCTION
16	FUNDAMENTALS
22	KINEMATICS
44	ASSEMBLIES
54	DYNAMICS
68	VISUAL EFFECTS
82	STACKING
108	ACCESSORIES
118	& BEYOND

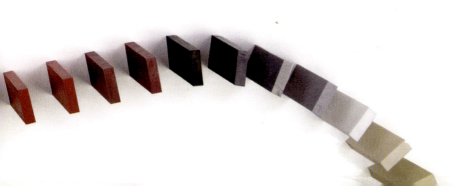

Origins

The actual starting point in the history of dominoes isn't completely certain. Evidence suggests that Egypt was the origin of dominoes, as the earliest known domino set was found in the ancient Egyptian King Tutankhamen's tomb. King Tut reigned in Egypt during the 18th Egyptian Dynasty, around 1355 BC, and the game set is on display at the Egyptian Museum in Cairo.

Despite the Egyptian evidence, many believe the Chinese were the inventors of the game in the 12th century, as early as 1120 A.D. Keung T'ai Kung was believed to have created the game to keep his soldiers awake and energized during their watches.

Hundreds of years later dominoes were introduced into Europe around the 18th century. Shortly after, France started producing two types of domino puzzles. In the first, the player was given a pattern and asked to place tiles on it in such a way that the ends matched. In the second type, the player was given a pattern and asked to place tiles based on arithmetic properties of the pieces, usually totals of lines of tiles and tile halves, similar to modern domino games today.

So when did people start stacking and toppling dominoes as we do now?

While we can't prove it, we believe that cavemen were stacking and toppling rocks like dominoes, and maybe aliens joined in on the fun! How else could the half-collapsed speed wall scientists call Stonehenge be explained?

In modern times, stacking and toppling dominoes wasn't popularized in large scale until the 1970's and has been growing ever since. Today, dominoes have been manufactured specifically for stacking and toppling and have been advanced over time due to technological advancements that make them more balanced, symmetrical, and colorful. These improvements make them easier to use, allow for higher stacking, longer toppling runs, and enable more complex tricks.

Today, whether people build dazzling domino displays in their homes for family and friends, or film them for the world to see online, these experiences spread the joy of dominoes and inspire the builders of tomorrow. While the future of domino toppling is yet to be seen, we look forward to what it holds, for our children, and our children's children.

Domino Physics

How do dominoes work?...

A toppling domino is a rectangular prism, usually twice as tall as it is wide, that is used in transferring a small amount of energy from one point to another. Toppling dominoes helps us understand Newton's First Law of Motion which states:

"An object at rest, stays at rest and an object in motion, stays in motion with the same speed and in the same direction unless acted upon by an unbalanced force."

In other words, a domino at rest will stay at rest until another force acts on it and a domino in motion will remain in motion until another force causes it to stop. Every domino run and system is a direct and fun example of this law. Tipping a domino is the force that removes the domino from rest, putting it in motion, and gravity, in combination with the friction created by the floor, is the force that stops it.

Dominoes can be linked in a system of reactions that are called "runs." A domino run usually consists of dominoes set up in a line that are close enough together that each domino falling will collide into the next, hence creating a chain reaction of motion until it reaches the end. These systems can be simple in nature, such as a straight line, or with tricks and turns that can reach a level of complexity that reaches the infinite.

Dominoes have potential, or stored, energy in each of them. This energy is released as kinetic energy as they move and tip into each other. The act of setting up each domino gives it energy, that energy gets released as the dominoes fall. Heavier dominoes have more energy than lighter dominoes because they have more mass. A domino run is like a big battery of stored energy. This fact is a fun way to look at domino toppling because a person can store their own energy into the dominoes and then release it in a spectacular display of chain reactions.

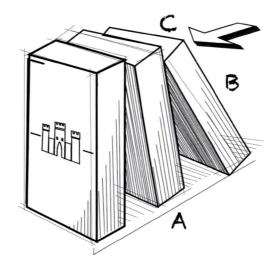

Choosing Dominoes

QUALITY

The quality and construction of dominoes is extremely important because if their edges are not straight and precise they will lean and fall over easily. It is also important that dominoes are balanced and symmetrical for maximum stability and performance. Edges and symmetry that vary, even slightly, will prevent the construction of large scale towers that reach to the ceiling and beyond! Without high quality dominoes, setting world records is nearly impossible.

SCALE / SIZE

The size of dominoes affects how much space is needed to build a run. If there is only a small area to build with, such as a counter top or desk, Mini Dominoes are a good choice as relatively large runs can still be made. If there is more building space, such as a table or floor, Pro Dominoes are the ultimate choice for topplers worldwide. When it comes to knocking down structures and building huge setups, larger dominoes, like the XL Dominoes are a great choice. XL Dominoes are large, stable, and make an excellent block for young builders. Regardless of the size of the domino, each can perform most, if not all, of the tricks in this book.

WEIGHT

The weight affects how stable a run or 3D build can be. A heavier domino is more stable when placing and building runs and structures. Lighter dominoes are easier to move around and are more cost effective when many are needed. Lighter dominoes can be tipped with greater ease by heavier dominoes. There are some setups that require both heavy and light dominoes to create neat tricks and effects.

COLORS

Some of the best domino falls in the world include the most visual effects and color coordination. With the right colors, dominoes turn into artwork, and can match characters, people, logos, pictures, and more. Pro Dominoes have the largest color selection in the world. Various domino styles, like Glow in the Dark, Neon, and Clear Dominoes create cool glowing, reflective, and transparent visual effects in domino runs.

TEXTURE

The texture of the domino effects the way it falls and slides. A "slick" domino will slide more easy on most surfaces and will actually topple faster. Whereas a more "grippy" domino will fall slower, lengthening the time of enjoyment, and will hold certain angles better. For example, a Lightning Run (p.19) is easier to build, with a domino that "grips" better.

UNIQUE DOMINOES

For even more creative and unique runs consider using Electro Dominoes, Mini Micro Dominoes, and Kinetic Planks. These offer flashing lights and large scale differences to the standard sizes of dominoes. This wild array of sizes allows for truly unique setups and challenges that really push the capabilities of the builder.

PRO

Precision made, top choice for schools, families, and professionals worldwide.

Dimensions:
Length: 48mm
Width: 24mm
Thickness: 7.5mm
Weight: 8.5g
Stability: ★★★★★
Balance: ★★★★★
Structures: ★★★★★
Gripability: ★★★★★
Color selection: 60+

KINETIC

Build in Pro-Scale with an eco friendly design and great performance.

Dimensions:
Length: 48mm
Width: 24mm
Thickness: 7.5mm
Weight: 4.4g
Stability: ★★★
Balance: ★★★★★
Structures: ★★★
Gripability: ★★
Color selection: 6+

ELECTRO

Topple activated, super-bright LED light up dominoes.

Dimensions:
Length: 48mm
Width: 24mm
Thickness: 7.5-12mm
Weight: 5.7g-9.3g
Stability: ★★★★★
Balance: ★★★★
Structures: ★★★★
Gripability: ★★★
Color selection: 4

MINI

Action in nearly 8X less space! Perfect for desktop fun and travel.

Dimensions:
Length: 24mm
Width: 12mm
Thickness: 4mm
Weight: 1.14g
Stability: ★★★
Balance: ★★★★
Structures: ★★★
Gripability: ★★★★
Color selection: 30+

KINETIC PLANKS

2.5x the length of Pro-Scale dominoes. Excellent for stacking and building structures and chain reactions.

Dimensions:
Length: 120mm
Width: 24mm
Thickness: 7.5mm
Weight: 9.7g
Stability: ★★
Balance: ★★★★★
Structures: ★★★★★
Gripability: ★★
Color selection: 16+

XL DOMINOES

Quickly build huge runs and structures. Uniquely builds with an integrated connection system.

Dimensions:
Length: 96mm
Width: 48mm
Thickness: 15mm
Weight: 30g
Stability: ★★★★★
Balance: ★★★★
Structures: ★★★
Gripability: ★
Color selection: 10+

MINI MICRO

The ultimate challenge! These are the official world record scale mini dominoes.

Dimensions:
Length: 10mm
Width: 5mm
Thickness: 2mm
Weight: 0.1g
Stability: ★
Balance: ★★★★
Structures: ★
Gripability: ★★★★
Color selection: 6+

NOTE: All domino images shown above, are all accurately proportional to one another.

Building surfaces

Ideal surfaces are flat, level, and do not vibrate or jostle easily, such as a smooth floor. For large intricate and time consuming builds, a little prep work on the building surface can go a long way. Make sure to clean the surface to make sure it is free of dirt and debris. Small crumbs and other particles can cause dominoes to lean and become unbalanced, especially when building with Mini & Mini Micro dominoes. Surface texture affects the sound, speed, and how dominoes fall, just like the texture of the domino will affect how it falls. Dominoes will slide around more after falling, on a "slick" surface, which can affect some domino runs and tricks, so it is good to keep this in mind when stacking. Trial runs on different surfaces will give the best idea of how the dominoes will behave when falling.

Best Surfaces:
Hardwood floors
Laminate floors
Polished concrete
Tables
Counters

Good Surfaces:
Tile
Brick and stone
Furniture

"Can Work" Surfaces:
Tightly woven carpets or rugs
Book covers
Wooden boards
Carpet*

*Carpet is not ideal but sometimes it's your only option.
Here are a few ways to build on carpeted surfaces:

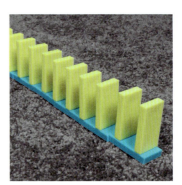

RAPID TRACK
Simply lay the rapid track across the carpet and knock the dominoes down!

STRAIGHT TRACK
Lay down some track and build away! It's easy!

DOMINO TRACK
Lay dominoes flat on the carpet and set up dominoes on top of those flat dominoes.

Placing Dominoes

When placing dominoes, the distance between them can vary which changes the speed, power, and capabilities of the falling dominoes. Placing a run of dominoes with a larger gap between each one will make the domino run take longer to fall overall, whereas placing smaller gaps between each one will decrease the time of the overall fall. If the gaps are too close, the dominoes will not have enough space to topple the next domino and the run will stop. If the gap is to large, the domino will not reach the next one, and the run will stop as well.

To get the most power out of a domino tipping, it should hit the next domino at about a 50° to 60° angle from the ground. This extra force helps knock down walls, towers, and larger dominoes with greater reliability.

Making turns in a domino run requires extra placement care since each domino needs to be placed by hand. For a continuous turn or corner, the dominoes should have smaller gaps between them for better reliability. Sharp or abrupt turns in a run have a higher risk of failing, so proper placement will help reliability, especially for beginner builders.

Many domino tricks require delicate placement and a steady hand to keep from mistakenly toppling a domino run or build. As the saying goes, "practice makes perfect", and some of these tricks take just that. There are, however, tools that make domino stacking much easier.

The template is a tool that aligns dominoes in a straight line and will keep the dominoes from falling until removed. This makes setups faster and easier for domino runs, fields, walls, and towers. Templates work with: Pro, Kinetic, Mini Dominoes and Planks. For smaller dominoes, a precision tool or tweezers make setups much easier as fingers will get in the way.

When stacking towers and walls it is important to keep the build as square as possible to form a strong foundation to build on. If the foundation is not square and balanced the build will become more unstable the taller it gets. Small towers are fairly forgiving, so give it a try and have fun!

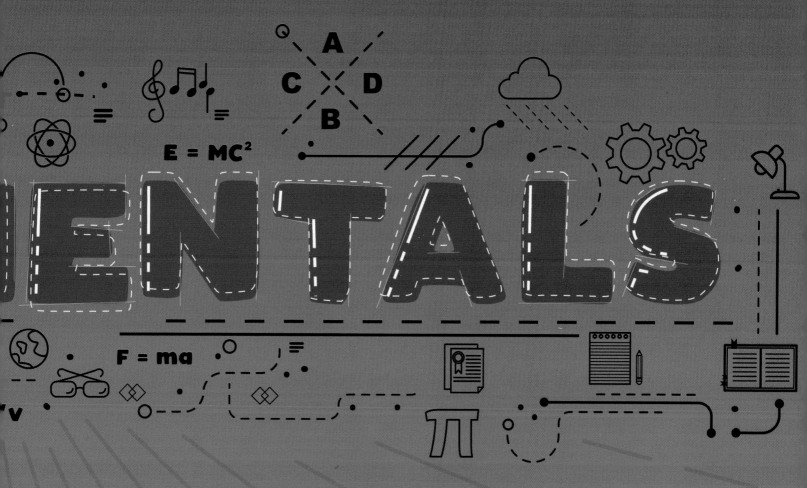

ENTALS

$$A$$
$$C \times D$$
$$B$$

$$E = MC^2$$

$$F = ma$$

Learn the basics and the core understanding of domino toppling. Did you know? A single domino can knock down another that is 1.5 times it's own size!

BASIC LINE

The most basic is sometimes the best!

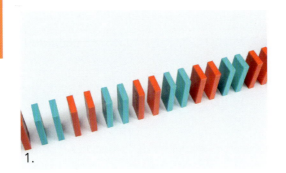

1.

2.

Set up dominoes vertically at a distance where they will topple each other.

Try setting them up horizontally (on their side) for a different visual appearance.

SIMPLE CURVE

Straight lines are fun, but curves are awesome!

1.

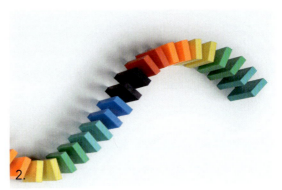

2.

Curves are a simple way to add more movement to your setup. Keep dominoes a bit closer than usual on the turns.

Can you make a slithering snake?

SPIRAL

Creates a neat spinning effect as the dominoes topple from the inside or the outside.

1.

2.

Start setting dominoes vertically from the center, and work your way out in a spiraling motion.

Dominoes can be set up vertically side by side in a similar spiraling effect.

FLOW SPIRAL

Creates a spiral that topples through the center and back out to continue the run.

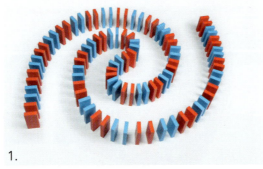

1.

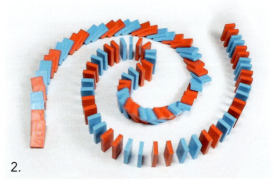

2.

The Flow Spiral is set up so that the domino toppling continues after the spiral is completed.

Flow Spiral in motion.

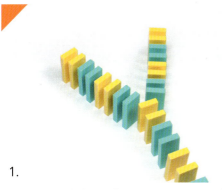

1.

Build a single line, then position two dominoes off the corners of the last domino in that line to create multiple toppling runs.

2.

Watch the dominoes split off in separate directions.

BASIC SPLIT

Use a split to add on another run for twice the fun!

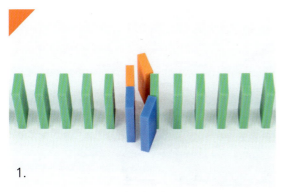

1.

Split one run into multiple directions.

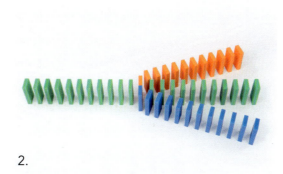

2.

Add dominoes to gradually split lines.

MULTI SPLIT

Your runs can transition into any number of lines.

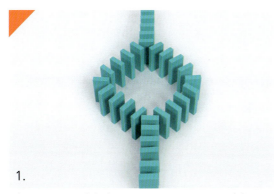

1.

The Diamond Split is an easy way to add some fun to a straight domino line.

2.

Watch the dominoes split off and meet back up into one line.

DIAMOND SPLIT

Simple way to add some flare to your runs.

1.

This is very important! Create a gap in your runs when setting up long chain reactions to protect your hard work in case of accidents.

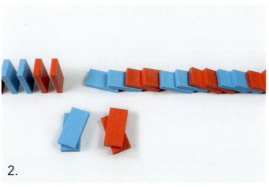

2.

The rest of your setup survives in case one part topples. Don't forget to fill them before starting the run.

SAFETY GAP

In case of an accident. Safety Gaps will prevent the loss of the entire setup.

TURN

Depending on your space or visual preference, you can setup 90° turns in many different ways.

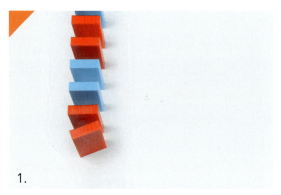

1.

Gradually angle the next domino towards the direction you want the line to go.

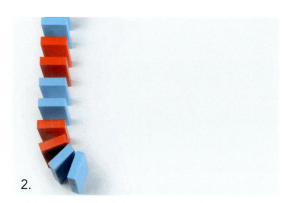

2.

Add three angled dominoes until you get a 90° turn.

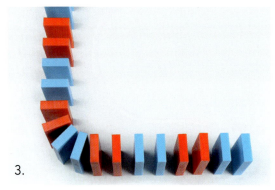

3.

Your turn is now complete and able to continue its journey.

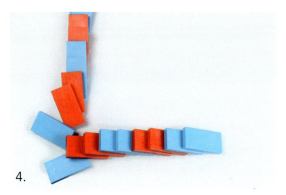

4.

This is a great minimalist way to turn sharply.

LEANING TURN

Fancy 90° turn with a leaning domino inside of it.

1.

Set up the sides first, then insert and angle the middle domino, then place a domino on top to complete.

2.

Dominoes fall in the direction of the inner angled domino.

TIGHT TURN

Use this when you need a tight corner. Make turns more gradual to increase reliability and decrease domino spread.

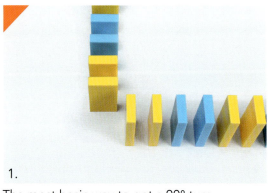

1.

The most basic way to get a 90° turn.

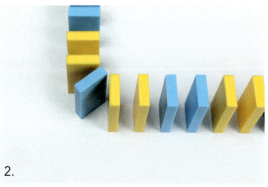

2.

Add one 45° angled domino to complete the turn.

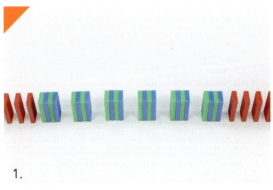

1.

Place groups of dominoes together with gaps between them. Works with up to 5 dominoes thick.

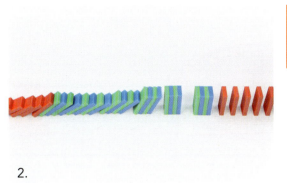

2.

This creates a different sound and falling effect.

SEGMENTS

Creates a cool effect of falling pillars with speed changes.

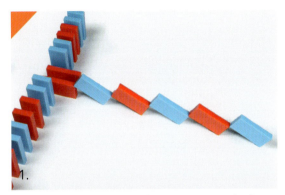

1.

This setup falls lighting fast. Set up each domino with the corners barely touching the one in the front.

2.

The dominoes typically fall standing up and have a different sound when they fall.

LIGHTNING RUN

This way of stacking creates a very rapidly falling chain reaction while creating a very different sound.

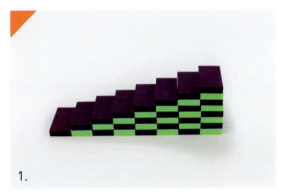

1.

Stack flat dominoes as shown above.

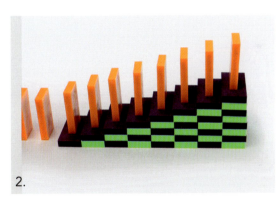

2.

Add dominoes on each step.

DOMINO STAIRS

Simply stack dominoes into a staircase to go up.

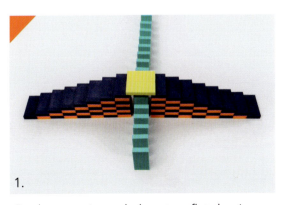

1.

Stack two stairs and place two flat dominoes across the gap. Bridge needs to be at least eight dominoes high for an underneath pass.

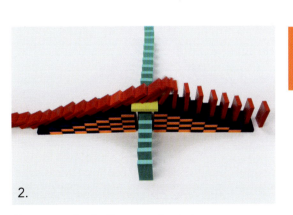

2.

These can be built around existing runs to easily bridge over them.

DOMINO BRIDGES

Simply lay a flat domino or plank across the gap of two stairs to build a perfect bridge.

construct

MATICS

sign

build

Tricks and setups involving pivots, mechanics, rotation, and motion to create awesome effects that really move.

BASIC CROSSOVER

Crossovers are tricks that allow your domino runs to cross through each other and continue on their path.

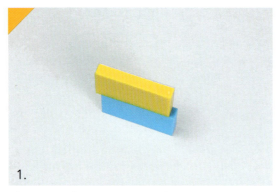

1.

Place one domino on its side and another on top leaving a little bit hanging over.

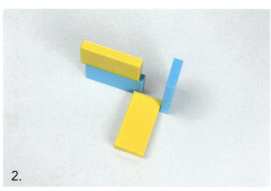

2.

Use a flat domino to measure proper distance. Stand a domino up on end.

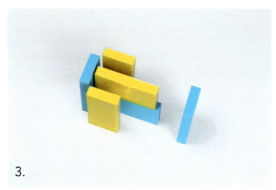

3.

Add dominoes on each long side of the stacked dominoes.

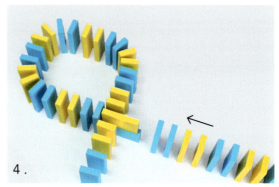

4.

You can add domino lines before or after you add your crossover pieces.

SECURE CROSSOVER

A more stable version of the Basic Crossover.

1.

Place three dominoes flush and horizontally next to each other.

2.

Add two dominoes centered on top of the three.

3.

Add dominoes to each side of the stacked dominoes.

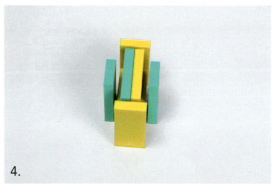

4.

Add vertical dominoes to each end of the stacked dominoes.

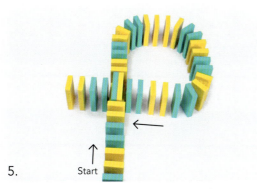

5.

Start

Build a lead-in line and topple it in the direction that will hit the end of the stacked dominoes first, not the sides.

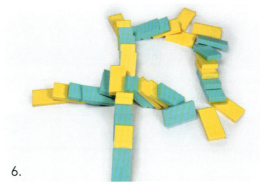

6.

Observe the after-effect of the dominoes toppled.

SECURE CROSSOVER (CONT.)

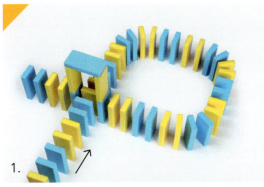

1.

Setup a small tower that bridges over the first line that will topple when the line comes around to the crossover point.

2.

You can see how the dominoes fall over the line.

SPEED CROSSOVER

Crossover that utilizes a toppling bridge with an underpass.

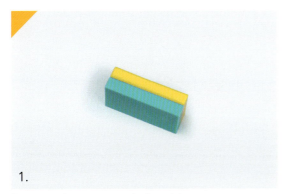

1.

Set two dominoes side by side.

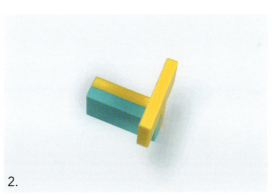

2.

Place a domino on the end of the two below it.

PISTON SWITCH

In a scenario where you don't have a domino switch accessory, you can make your own using only dominoes.

The switch allows the domino run to smoothly reverse direction.

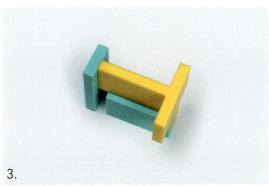

3.

Place another on top in the direction of the two below it and one behind it for support.

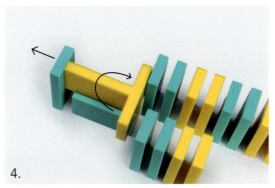

4.

The domino connecting the two lines will pivot and allow your domino lines to change directions.

THE REVERSE

Fairly unstable trick but it allows your dominoes to quickly change directions.

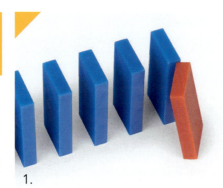

1.

Lean the domino at the end of the first line facing the opposite direction.

2.

Add the second line fairly close to the leaning domino.

THE CHUTE

The Chute is a fun and different way to send one domino into another. This trick is easy to set up using just a few dominoes.

1.

Start building your platform, with two dominoes on bottom, and one on top.

leave small gap from edge

2.

Add two dominoes on the right hand side then one horizontally stacked domino on the top.

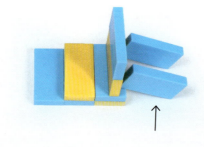

3.

Add another domino on top of the horizontally stacked domino. Then, add two leaning dominoes on the edge.

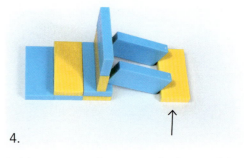

4.

Add a support domino at the base of the two leaning dominoes.

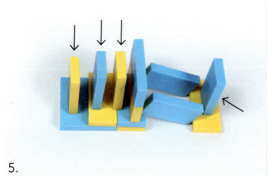

5.

Add vertical dominoes to both chutes sitting on top of the flat dominoes. Your chute unit is complete.

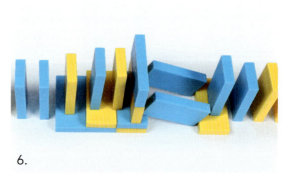

6.

You can chain multiple chutes together.

Pushes dominoes into the next segment for a neat falling effect.

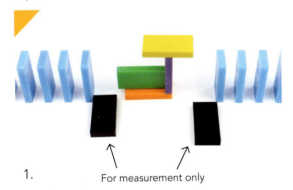

1.

Lay dominoes flat, one domino length apart. Set one horizontal then one vertical domino on top of the flat domino. Add lead-in & lead-out.

2.

Topple from left to right to watch the dominoes jitter into each other.

Add that extra punch to your run.

1.

Repeat step one of The Jitter. Then, place a flat domino on top of the vertical one. Add lead-in and lead-out lines.

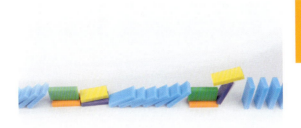

2.

Build another line after the trick and add as many Jitter Hitters as desired. Topple left to right.

In this trick, colored dominoes will fall like synchronized swimmers in a show of coordinated color stacking.

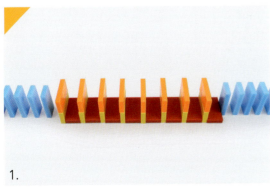

1.

Set up flat dominoes flush to one another. On top of them, set horizontal dominoes on the edge of the one below it.

2.

The dominoes will topple flat, laying next to each other.

Same as The Synchronizer, but with two horizontal dominoes stacked on one another.

1.

Set 2 dominoes on top of each other horizontally with one domino flat between each segment.

2.

Creates a falling/tipping effect that will slightly slow down the run.

THE COMEBACK

A fun, unique way to topple your dominoes twice in a single run!

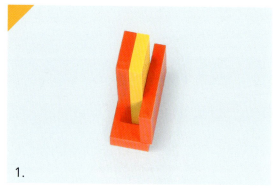

1.

Place one domino flat, two vertical on top, and one horizontal on top hanging over the edge just slightly.

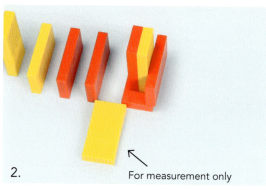

2.

For measurement only

Build a lead-in line, with dominoes placed horizontally, then space the last domino closer so that when it topples it barely touches.

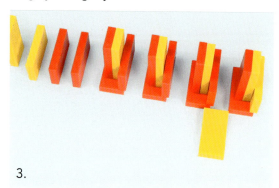

3.

Continue step one until you have four stacks each spaced apart, just smaller than the width of a domino.

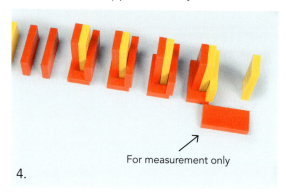

4.

For measurement only

Continue your line at less than a domino distance away from the last stack.

5.

From the corner of the last stack, start placing dominoes at a gradual angel.

6.

Begin building your curve by placing two flat dominoes perpendicularly facing the first stack.

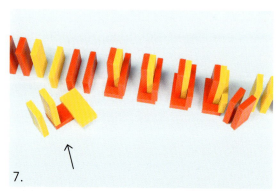

7.

Add one domino on the end of the bottom flat domino and then finish placing the curve.

8.

Your trick is now complete. Topple from left to right on the straight domino line and watch the trick unfold.

The Missing Link utilizes gaps and momentum to create a last second completion to continue a domino setup.

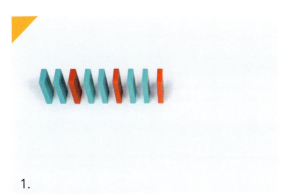

1.

Start your standard line.

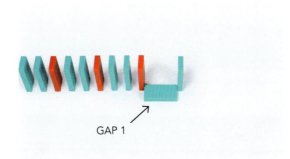

GAP 1

2.

Continue your line but leave a gap the length of a domino. Remove flat (measurement) domino.

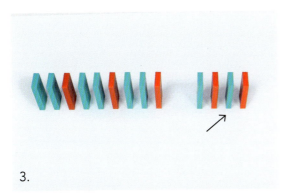

3.

Set up 4 dominoes or so, then create space for another gap.

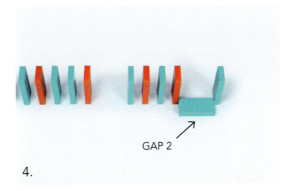

GAP 2

4.

Another gap.

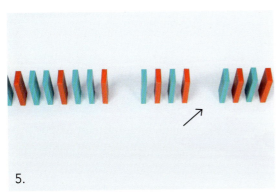

5.

Continue line after second gap.

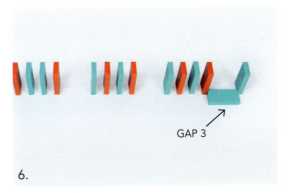

GAP 3

6.

Make another gap.

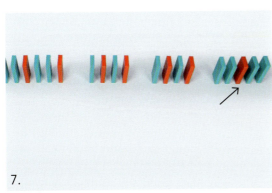

7.

Line continued..

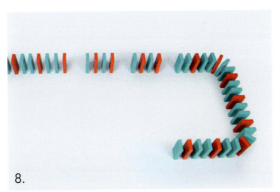

8.

Continue line with two turns.

In this trick the run will push dominoes into future gaps that unless filled, would stop the run from working. It's so cool!

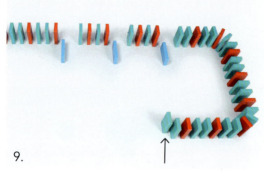

9.

Stop the domino line when it seems parallel with Gap 3. Add horizontal dominoes beside each gap.

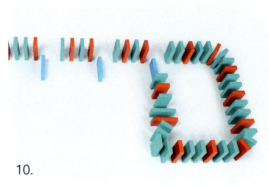

10.

Build a line towards Gap 3.

11.

Add dominoes until parallel to Gap 2. Repeat step 10 to add another joining line on the next gap.

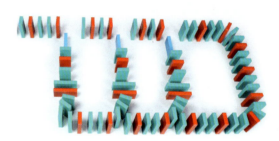

12.

Repeat previous step to make the last line.

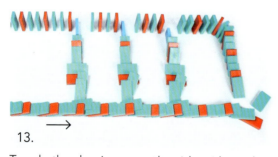

13.

Topple the dominoes on the side without the gaps.

14.

The line that connects the outer lines will push the horizontal dominoes to fill the gap and allow the run to continue.

COLOR FLIPPER

This trick gives the illusion of your line changing colors.

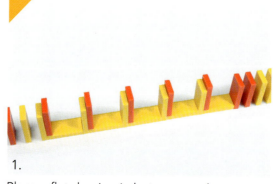

1.

Place a flat domino in between each vertical domino. Then place an additional vertical domino up against the verticals.

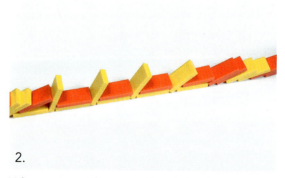

2.

When using different colored dominoes, they will appear to change color, when they topple.

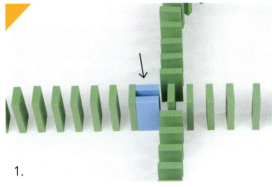

1.

Put two dominoes sideways and run your crossover line slightly past them in the direction they are going to fall.

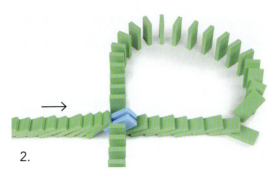

2.

Topple from the left and watch as it wraps and comes back around to continue the run.

LATERAL CROSSOVER

Make a crossover by using two dominoes in a sideways fashion that will lean first and then topple from the side.

LOOP & SWOOP

Loop & Swoop is a combination of awesome and function. This trick can crossover as many links as desired.

1.

Place two vertical dominoes with a gap between them, then place a flat domino butted up against them on either side. Repeat.

2.

Place the flipper dominoes up against the preceding two.

3.

Layout lines leading into the crossover points, for the crossover effect.

4.

Continue laying out crossover lines until they merge into one line.

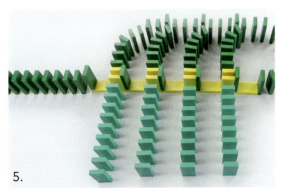

5.

Build lead-out lines to complete the crossover and continue the toppling.

6.

Topple from left to right and watch it loop and swoop.

LIGHTNING BOLT

Transitions from the Lightning Run to keep toppling dominoes.

1.

Set up a lighting run (pg.19).

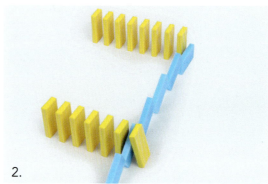

2.

Set up a vertical line perpendicular to the lightning run on one side and on the other side lean a domino against the lightning run.

LIGHTNING STORM

This transition can be used to make all the dominoes fall from the same direction.

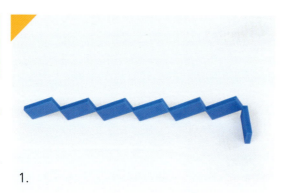

1.

With a perpendicular starting block, create a lightning run (pg. 19).

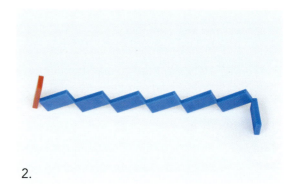

2.

Place a domino leaning up against the last domino.

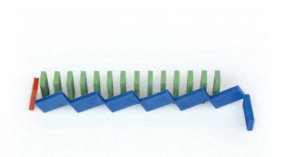

3.

Place a line in front of the leaning domino to transition. Be sure to keep the start of the run close to the leaning domino.

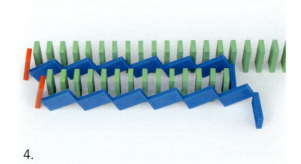

4.

Repeat steps one and two on the back side, followed by a basic lead-out line.

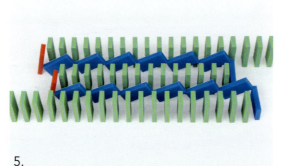

5.

Build a lead-in line.

6.

Topple from left to right.

Creates a back
and forth effect
with dominoes
falling into the
next run.

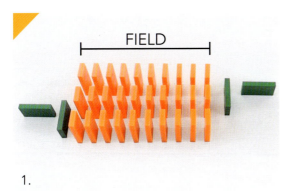

1.

Create a center "Field" and start the ends as shown.

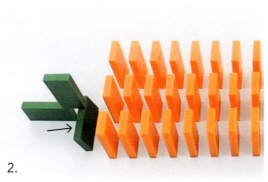

2.

Tilt the inside domino back slightly when placing the domino on top.

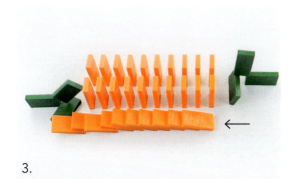

3.

Topple from the bottom line.

4.

This trick can be expanded to any size.

You really have
to build this
trick to see it
in action!

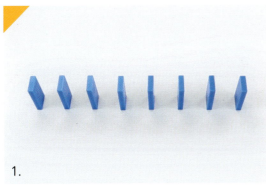

1.

Set up the baseline.

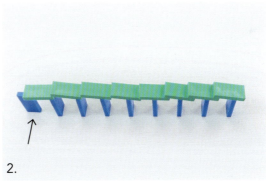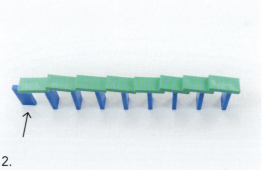

2.

Place a vertical domino perpendicular on the end of the run. Place dominoes on top overlapping each other.

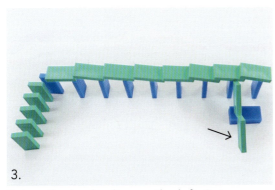

3.

Set up the lead-in line on the left. Set up a small lightning run leaning against the base line with 2 dominoes stacked underneath.

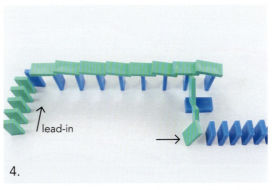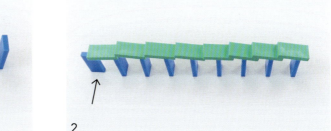

lead-in

4.

Build a lead-out line from the end of the lightning run with the first domino leaning slightly in the direction of the run.

PERGOLA

Travel up and over dominoes for some elevated horizontal toppling.

1.

Build two horizontal walls a domino width apart, place horizontal dominoes on top close together, build runs on each side.

2.

Topple from stairs on the right side and watch the dominoes race across the top.

COLONNADE

A fun top-heavy topple that falls simultaneously.

1.

Set up a lead-in on the left with 2 on top of 1 flat domino. Then set up 1 vertical domino with 1 flat on top. Continue building columns.

2.

All towers fall at exactly the same time. NOTE: this trick is limited on how many columns that can be toppled simultaneously.

LITTLE NUDGE

Instantly pushes the energy through the dominoes. Fun trick to put into your runs.

1.

Set one domino horizontally and another on top perpendicular. Continue building these with each one touching the next.

2.

Build a line on both sides. Dominoes will fall simultaneously and accelerate your line. NOTE: this trick is limited on length to work properly.

CLICK-CLACKS

Easy addition to change up the look and feel of your runs.

1.

Set up a normal line, then horizontal dominoes, then back to normal run. Place vertical dominoes against horizontal pieces.

2.

The end result falls neatly into place.

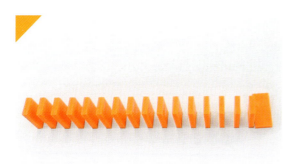

1.

Place a flat domino up against the last domino in the line.

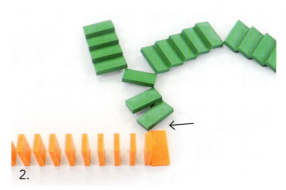

2.

Lean one corner of a domino flat onto the corner of the other flat dominoes. Continue this until desired length is reached.

SHEET LIGHTNING

Subtle effect. Dominoes must barely be placed on the preceding domino.

1.

Set up "π" towers fairly close together.

2.

Creates a staggered falling effect.

PI TOWERS

This setup adds a little wave and extra power behind your toppling.

1.

Line up dominoes with the last one slightly offset. Lean a domino up against the offset one.

2.

Lean more horizontal dominoes up against each other, with the dominoes leaning towards the preceding domino.

SNAKE RUN

Weave away your dominoes with this trick and listen for the "Ooo's" and "Ahh's".

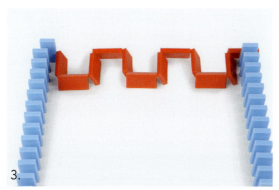

3.

The greater the lean, the more reliable the trick will be.

4.

This trick creates a neat weaving effect.

SPARKS

A fun way to spark up a line in your run!

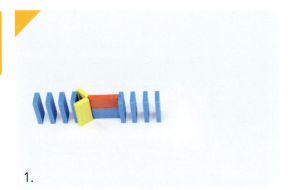

1.

Place a "V" after the lead-in line, followed by two horizontal stacked dominoes that are against the "V". Add vertical dominoes.

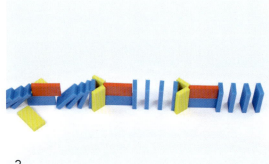

2.

Make sure the lead vertical domino is touching the stack. Then, place as many Sparks as desired in sequence. Topple left to right.

SPRINGBOARD CORNER

Makes a nice, clean, and easy corner that has no spread to accidentally knock down another part of your run.

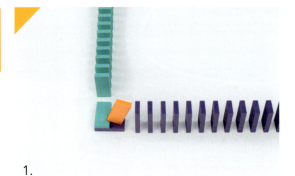

1.

Place a domino halfway on top of the bottom domino. Place vertical domino on top of both.

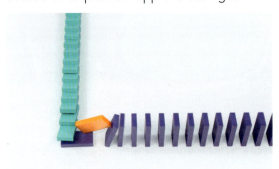

2.

Build a lead-in line and start toppling from the right. Easy corner effect. No spread.

THE SEA SERPENT

Spice up your horizontal runs with this trick.

1.

Make a run of horizontal dominoes and leave gaps. Bridge the gaps with a perpendicular horizontal domino.

2.

Watch the tipping action begin.

CLUSTER

Create some delayed falling action in your run with this trick.

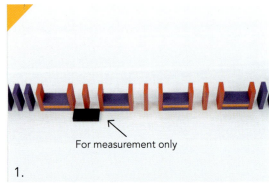

For measurement only

1.

One unit is three stacked dominoes with a vertical domino touching each end.

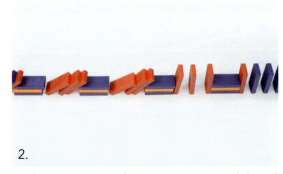

2.

Each unit tips into the next creating a delayed reaction between each topple.

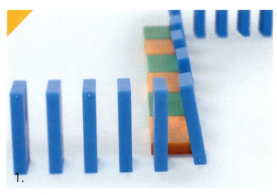

1. Lay out a line of flat dominoes. Lean a domino to just-about-falling on every joining line.

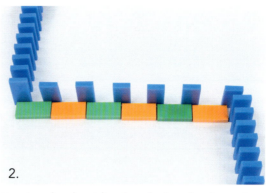

2. Create a lead-out line by placing dominoes in front of the last leaning domino. Watch as each domino falls flat, triggering the next.

STANCHION

Each leaning domino will fall flat mysteriously motivating the next leaning domino to fall.

1. Stack dominoes as shown in the image above.

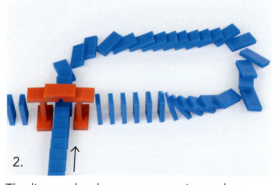

2. The line under the crossover unit needs to topple first before the crossover line occurs.

PAGODA CROSSOVER

Add oriental flare to your run with this easy-to-set-up trick!

1. From a line, place a domino horizontally and lean another domino's corner up against its side.

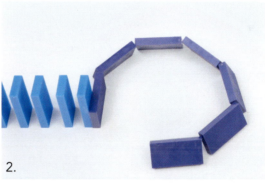

2. Continue leaning dominoes until your line starts coiling. A more gradual coil works best.

COBRA COILS

Create a fast, horizontally toppling circle reaction to add movement and style to your line.

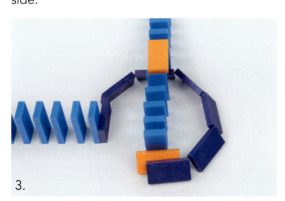

3. To continue the run, place dominoes vertically against the last horizontal domino.

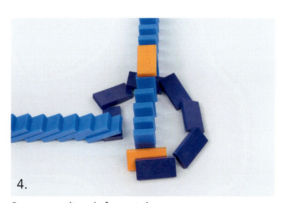

4. Start toppling left to right.

FORKED LIGHTNING

Split a lightning run into multiple lightning runs.

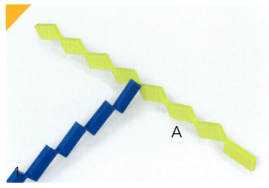

1.

Form a lightning run (pg. 19)(A). Form lightning run (B) by placing the lead domino at any low point on lighting run (A)

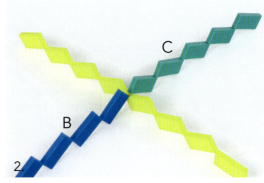

2.

Place an additional lightning run (C) in the opposing direction of lighting run (B).

LATERAL WAVE

Easy to set up and fun to watch all the dominoes fall in place resting on each other.

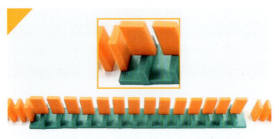

1.

Place one flat & one horizontal domino and repeat for desired length. Place side-by-side dominoes on top.

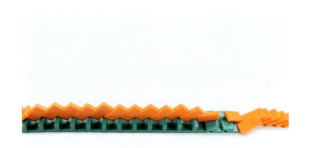

2.

Dominoes will rest neatly on each other. This can also work as a safety gap if top dominoes are placed later.

REVERTERS

You might think the stacked dominoes will fall the wrong way, but they keep the run going back and forth. This trick can be used in field toppling.

1.

Place a domino horizontally and a little offset in front of your run.

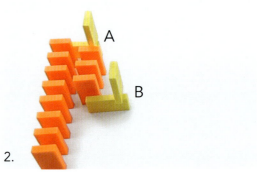

2.

(A) Place a domino on top of first horizontal domino, continue run. (B) Then repeat step one to reverse back.

3.

Make the trick as long as you would like and switch back and forth as many times as you would like.

4.

Dominoes will reverse fall, switching the directions each time.

Watch your runs topple out from the center like a zipper un-zipping with this delicate trick.

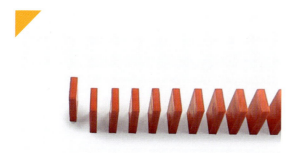

1.

Create a lead-in line with the last domino slightly offset.

2.

Lean the next two dominoes as shown in the image above

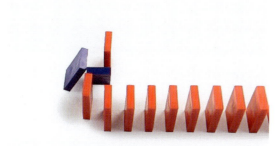

3.

Place a vertical domino in front of the last leaning domino.

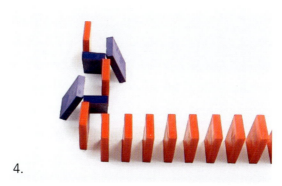

4.

Repeat steps 2 and 3 until you are content.

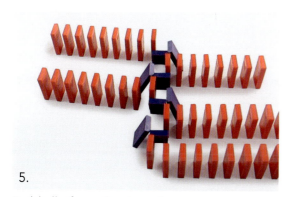

5.

Build all of your lead-out lines.

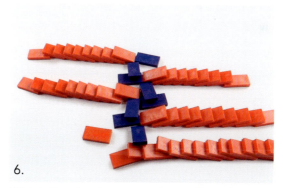

6.

Watch the dominoes topple out from the center back and forth.

Simple trick that adds some flare to an otherwise basic run.

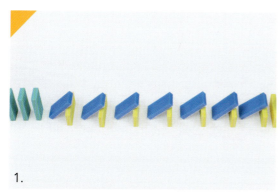

1.

Place horizontal dominoes at almost a domino length apart. Lay leaning dominoes in between and continue the run.

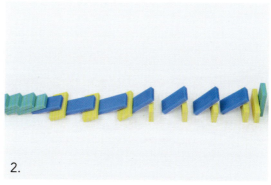

2.

Dominoes will topple neatly and will give a basic line some flare. A good way to add a fun colorful effect.

SURFBOARD SWITCH

An easy way to go back and forth with horizontal dominoes.

1.

Run dominoes horizontally. Place the last domino offset. Start next line and place a domino on top of both.

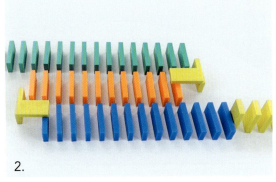

2.

Continue trick until desired length and then repeat step one.

HIGH HURDLES

Add some high falling action with this simple stacking method.

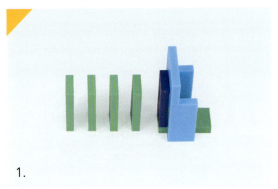

1.

Place two dominoes vertically with one laying flat in between, one vertically on the end of the flat one, and one on top horizontally.

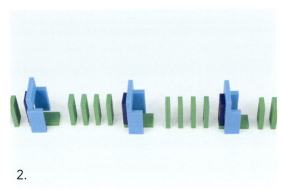

2.

Place four dominoes in between hurdles and topple from left to right.

SUPERBOLT

A lightning run with twice the falling action and fun.

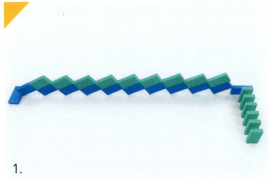

1.

Set up your normal lightning run (pg. 19) with a safety domino. Then stack the next row on top for more toppling action.

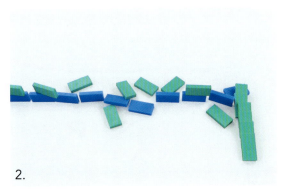

2.

Use the Superbolt to supercharge your run.

COLUMN DROP

It doesn't look like it should work, but try it and watch each stack collide into the next.

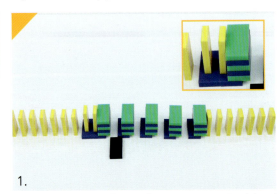

1.

Lay one domino flat with two on top. Build columns six dominoes high right next to the first flat domino with the bottom domino offset.

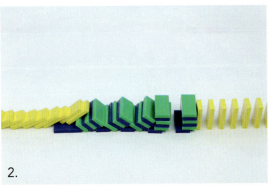

2.

Continue columns about a domino's width apart. Topple and watch the columns collide.

1.

Stack dominoes as shown in the image above.

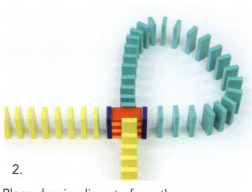

2.

Place domino lines to form the crossover.

COLUMN CROSSOVER

This is a sturdy and easy crossover method. Crossovers are helpful when space is limited.

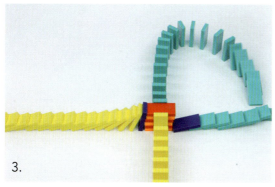

3.

Start toppling from the left.

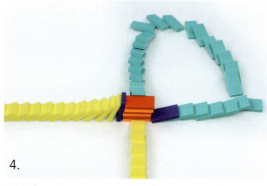

4.

Watch as it crosses over, then comes back around to close the loop.

1.

Start by laying out flat dominoes for the base of the crossover. Add a second layer.

2.

Place three horizontal dominoes on top, with two perpendicular ones in between.

COASTER RAIL

Use this method of crossover if you need to crossover multiple times in one location or if you just want your run to look awesome.

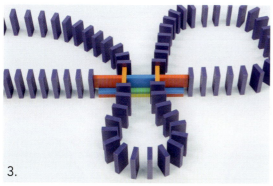

3.

Make sure ends of the run are touching the Coaster Rail. Build lines and loops out from the perpendicular center dominoes.

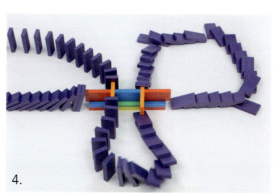

4.

Start toppling from left and watch it zig zag its way through the middle. This can be used in many different ways.

SPACE SHIPS

Dominoes will push and slide each domino into the next set. An easy fun effect.

1.

Set two dominoes horizontally and one vertically between them. Add a horizontal domino perpendicularly on top.

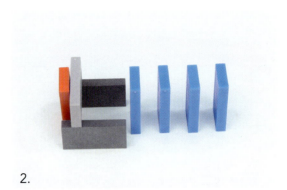

2.

Build a line in front of the Space Ship. Minimum recommendation is four dominoes.

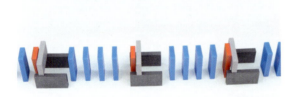

3.

Repeat step 1 and 2 until you are satisfied with the number of Space Ships you have, then build a lead-out line.

4.

The Space Ships in action.

V-BOOSTER

Add a boost to your run with this easy trick!

1.

Lay two dominoes horizontally in a "V" shape pointing in the direction the run will go. Then place a domino on top.

2.

Repeat step one until you reach the desired number of Boosters.

REVERSE V-BOOSTER

Dominoes topple in the reverse direction in this trick!

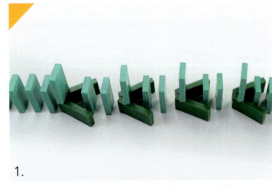

1.

Lay two dominoes horizontally in a "V" shape pointing against the direction the run will go. Place a domino on the point.

2.

Topple from left to right and watch as the dominoes boost in the reverse direction.

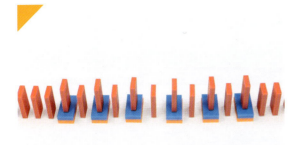

1.

Lay two dominoes flat and place a domino vertically on each stack.

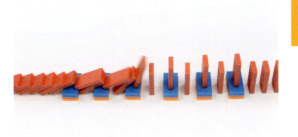

2.

Place dominoes between each stack.

RESONATOR

Easy way to have some vertical change in a basic line setup.

1.

Set up two horizontal walls parallel to each other.

2.

Set up vertical dominoes a domino's width apart between the walls.

RUNNING THE GAUNTLET

Slow down your run with this trick but make sure the dominoes between the walls are not too close together, or you won't make it through the gauntlet!

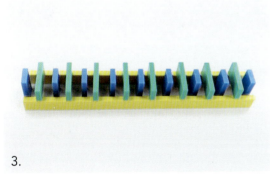

3.

Place horizontal dominoes across the wall between each standing domino all equally spaced apart.

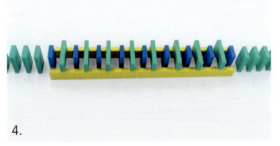

4.

Build your lead-in and lead-out lines. Watch it slow your run down in a sliding style.

$$F = \frac{gm_1 \, m_2}{d_2}$$

$b^2 = c^2$

A group of adjacent domino lines that completely cover a given area like a blanket. Fields (assemblies) are commonly used to spell out words, create images using different color dominoes, or create wave-like effects.

BASIC FIELD

This is a basic yet effective way to build a field and knock down a wave of dominoes all at once.

1.

Start your line to begin the field.

2.

Set two dominoes directly in front of your line, and then three.

3.

Four, five, etc. until you reach the width of the field you want to build.

4.

Maintain that width by putting the same number of dominoes in each row.

5.

Add as many rows as desired.

6.

These "assemblies" can be lined up next to each other to make a large field.

HORIZONTAL FIELD

Create a slower falling field by laying the dominoes sideways.

1.

Follow the same principles as the basic field, except lay dominoes on their side.

2.

Build your lead-in line and make sure they are closely spaced together to ensure they will all topple.

1.

Starting from a line, set two dominoes angled to form a triangle, then build circle lines keeping them close together.

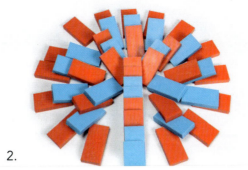

2.

Dominoes will fall in a beautiful circular display.

CIRCLE FIELD

End your setup with some fireworks by building a circular field that topples from the inside out.

FLAG POLE FIELD STARTER

These starters are nice when you want to enter the field from another angle as opposed to straight on.

1.

Set up three dominoes as depicted above.

2.

Repeat step one...

3.

Keep repeating step one until you reach the desired width of your field.

4.

Start building off of the angled dominoes to begin your field.

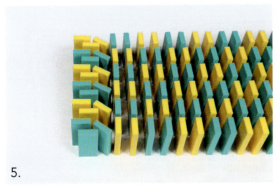

5.

The Flag Pole Field Starter is ready to go! Let 'em fly!

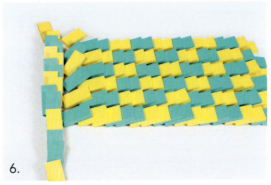

6.

Beautiful! Works very well in tight spaces and uses a minimal number of dominoes.

RECIPROCATING FIELD

Reciprocating Field is great for building in the middle of a domino setup or if you want your fields to topple slower and change directions.

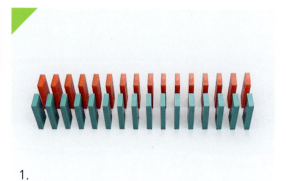

1.

Start building lines parallel to one another.

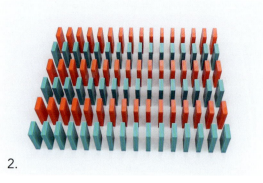

2.

Continue as many lines as you'd like until you are satisfied.

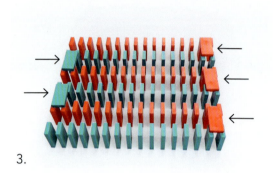

3.

Connect lines by placing one flat domino on each end bridging the gap.

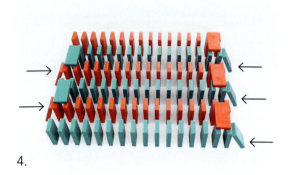

4.

Place leaning dominoes on the end of each line, alternating sides.

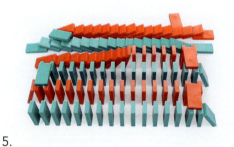

5.

Topple from the top and watch the dominoes topple back and forth.

6.

End result of a Reciprocating Field.

CHAIN LIGHTNING FIELD STARTER

This is a great way to topple fields while not taking up much room but can be very touchy. Stack with care.

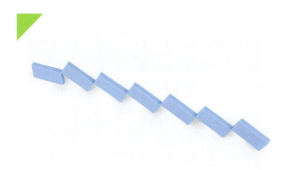

1.

Create a lightning run (pg. 19).

2.

Add the field trigger dominoes to the top corner of each diagonal domino and support it with a vertical domino.

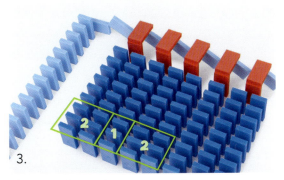

3.

Place an alternating pattern of two, one, two, dominoes in front of the trigger dominoes for proper spacing.

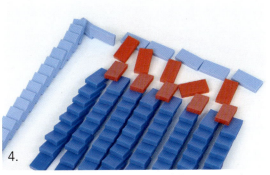

4.

The lightning run will rapidly fall causing the field to almost fall simultaneously.

POWER DIVE FIELD STARTER

Use this method to knock down a field in a dramatic way. It will knock down the field from only one side and doesn't take up much room.

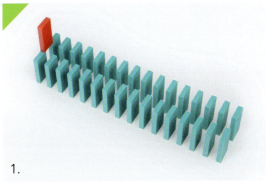

1.

Build two parallel lines, closer than a domino's width apart.

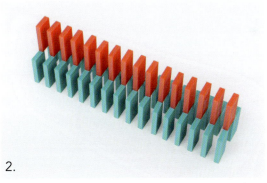

2.

Stack vertical dominoes on top, between the two lines, bridging the gap.

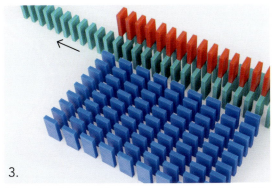

3.

Place lead-in and lead-outs in front of the side you want your field on. Then place field.

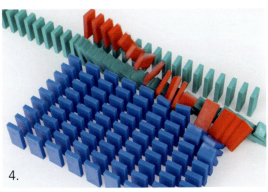

4.

Watch as the dominoes dive and start the field toppling.

MID-FIELD CROSSOVER

Works on narrow fields better as it is limited on how far it will work. It is good to practice a few times before putting it in an actual setup.

1. Set up a basic field leaving out one row in the middle. Place one domino off center and lean the others flush.

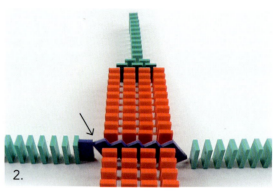

2. Overall set up. The leaning line will need to topple first.

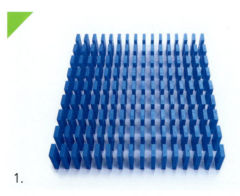

3. Leaning line toppled, notice the purple dominoes are facing the other direction.

4. This allows the field to continue.

CROSS FIELDS

Cross Fields topple dominoes at different directions at the same time.

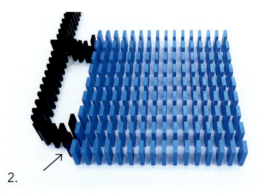

1. Build a field using straight lines to the desired size of field.

2. Build a lead-in line that spans to two dominoes from the single line to topple three of the domino lines.

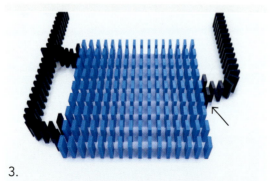

3. Build another line on the right side in the same way to topple three lines at a time.

4. Topple the lead-in lines at the same time and watch them cross and topple simultaneously.

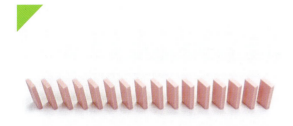

1.

Only need one lead-in line to topple an entire field. Sets up just like a normal field but angle each domino parallel to each other.

2.

Repeat step 1 until you reach your desired size.

If you want to try something new, make this style of field. It only needs one domino toppled for the whole field to topple.

3.

Add a lead-in line of dominoes. The field will look slightly slanted when done correctly.

4.

It creates a fan shape when falling. Put a lead-out line at the end to keep your run going.

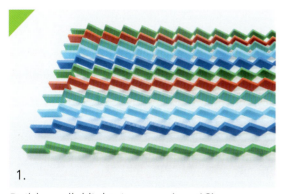

1.

Build parallel lightning runs (pg. 19).

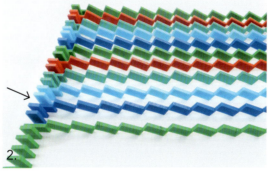

2.

Build a lead-in line with the horizontal dominoes. Topple the lead-in line and watch the Lightning Field begin.

The Lighting Field is an easy field to topple, but not the best for making pictures. It's one of the fastest falling fields and will create quite the ruckus when falling.

create picture fields

Picture fields look incredible in any domino run! The question is how do I make one? Well it's not as difficult as it seems, mostly just time consuming.

Things Needed:
Dominoes
Enough space to build
Time

Things That Are Helpful:
Template
Digital picture
Extra space to move on all sides

Designing fields can vary from small fields to world record size fields. Having a field size planned before starting helps when creating a picture field. Domino fields are like a bunch of small square segments, or pixels. The more "pixels" or dominoes in the picture the more detailed it will look. Also, in colorful or life-like pictures, having a large variety of colors will allow the domino fields to look more like the original picture.

Creating a picture from scratch can be tough, although not impossible (ask any artist), but there are easier ways to help any domino builder get an excellent looking domino field. There are programs available that will take a digital picture and convert it into a domino field layout that is easy to use. Following the layout row by row and placing the colors in the right order will yield a field that looks like the original digital image. There are also pixel pictures available online that have already been simplified to a grid of squares.

Normal Picture Field

This field is the most straightforward and easy to make. Lay down each layer with a template working from one end to the next. Use any of the field starter tricks to topple down the field.

Diamond Picture Field

This field style is as easy as the normal field as far as the picture layout goes. The difference will be that the picture will have a slight diagonal slant to it. The upside to this is the entire field can be started by a single domino line.

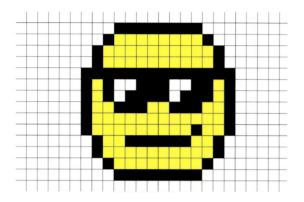 

Cross Picture Field

This field is more complicated. Decide how many rows you will use in each crossing path. This could be one row each or even half the rows in the field. Whatever you decide. Rows that are crossing each other need to be offset by exactly three dominoes, otherwise the picture will not look right when it is toppled. This offset of the rows will conceal the picture until the dominoes are toppled from both sides. See pictures for an example of this. This example picture uses about 5 rows in each crossing path.

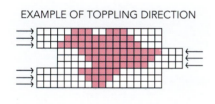

EXAMPLE OF TOPPLING DIRECTION

 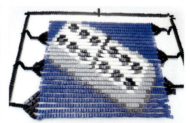

Alternating Picture Field

This field is like the cross field in the fact that there will be rows that are crossing past each other. The difference is each row will be opposing the next. Each of these rows needs the picture to be offset three dominoes or the picture will not look right when the dominoes topple. This field draws out the domino toppling time as each row will topple in sequence.

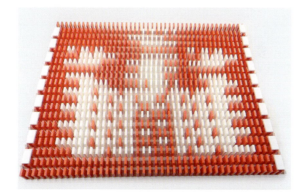 

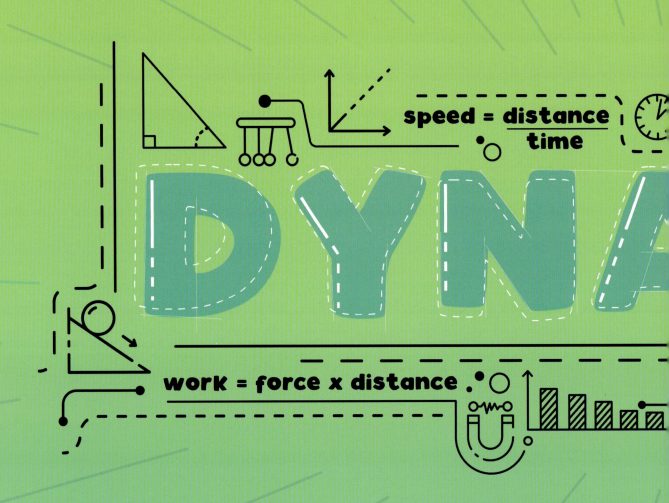

speed = $\dfrac{\text{distance}}{\text{time}}$

work = force x distance

MICS

$$F = ma$$

Momentum = mass x velocity

Setups that utilize momentum, gravity, ingenuity, and creative thinking to link energy together. This section includes flips, slides, rolls, jumps, and more!

HAND SPRING

Implementing a little bit of gymnastics into your domino movements is a great way to impress the crowd. Easy to set up and fun to watch.

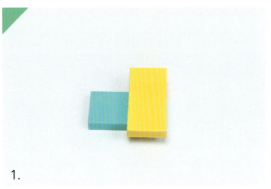

1.

Place one flat domino, another on top and flush with the edge of the bottom domino.

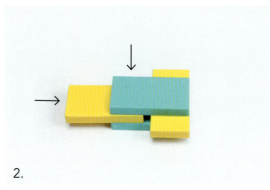

2.

Add a domino on the top, hanging off more than half. While holding it, place a domino on top flush with edge of the first domino.

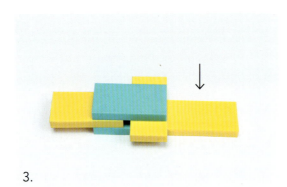

3.

Add a flat domino that touches the edge of the bottom domino.

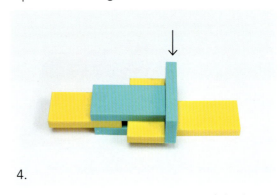

4.

Place a horizontal domino on top of the last domino.

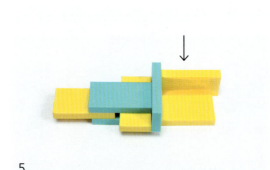

5.

Add a horizontal domino.

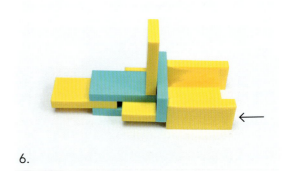

6.

Add a domino on the other side and a vertical domino on top.

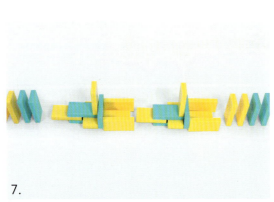

7.

Add as many Hand Springs as you'd like in your domino line.

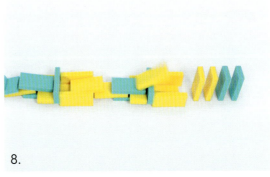

8.

The domino will hand spring over top of the horizontal domino and create a pleasing dynamic movement.

In this trick the dominoes fall slowly like a fainting goat.

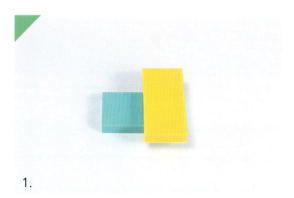

1.

Same as step one in Hand Spring.

2.

Same as step two in Hand Spring.

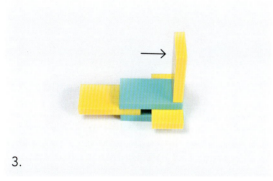

3.

Add a vertical domino flush to the backside of the stack. One fainting stack complete.

4.

Your lead in line should be a bit shorter than the length of a domino to hit the stack when falling.

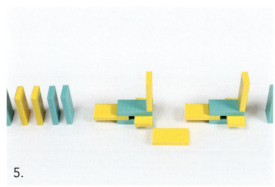

5.

Build as many fainting stacks as you'd like and watch the dominoes face plant into one another.

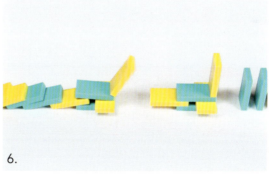

6.

Domino falling mid-action.

VERTICAL LIGHTNING

A neat diagonal trick that seems to fall in reverse.

1. Set up a basic line, offset one domino. Lean a domino up against that one. Continue leaning dominoes against each other in a diagonal line.

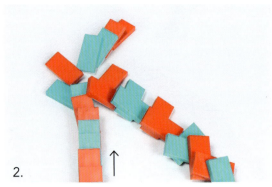

2. Once the straight line topples, the trick line will topple in reverse very quickly.

THE CLEAVER

You don't expect this split to work but it does.

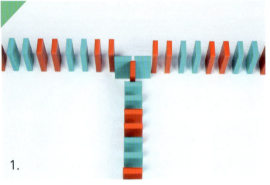

1. Set up one domino perpendicular to the basic line, with two in front, barely overlapping the corners, just outside the split.

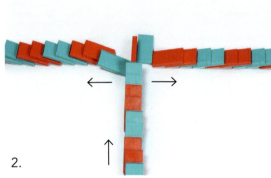

2. This is an easy way to get lines to travel in opposite directions simultaneously.

VERTIGO

This chain reaction triggers dominoes to slide across one another eventually hitting another domino line and changing directions while adding some excitement.

1. Lay several dominoes flat end to end.

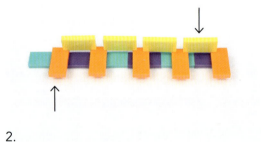

2. Place dominoes perpendicular on top of each flat domino, then horizontal dominoes on top.

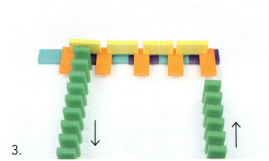

3. Add a lead-in line to the last flat domino. Add a lead-out line in front of the last horizontal domino.

4. Watch as the magic happens.

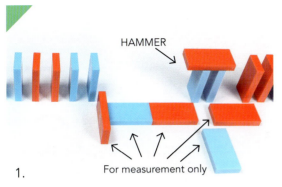

HAMMER

For measurement only

1.

Space the lead-in & lead-out lines as shown above. Place two dominoes close together on the bottom, with one flat on top.

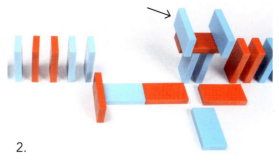

2.

Place two dominoes horizontally on top of the hammer.

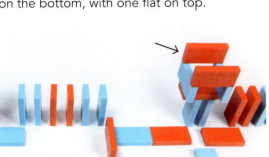

3.

Add two more dominoes on top.

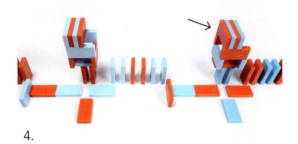

4.

Add four dominoes pressed together on the top left side.

5.

Remove "measurement only" dominoes.

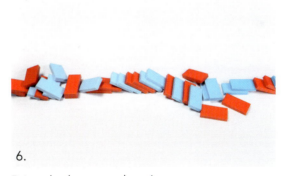

6.

Bring the hammer down!

THE HAMMER

The Hammer falls slowly but with a lot of force. It is great for toppling large structures or simply to continue a domino run.

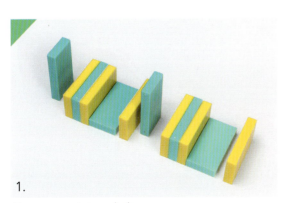

1.

Set up as pictured above.

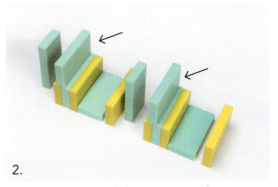

2.

Add one horizontal domino on each 3-stack.

HORIZONTAL FLIPS

Send your dominoes flipping!

HORIZONTAL FLIPS (CONT.)

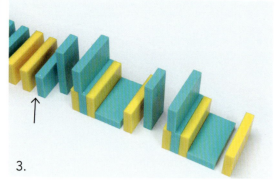

3.

Add your line to trigger the setup.

4.

Watch as the horizontal dominoes on top do front flips to propel the chain reaction forward.

STEAM ROLLER

Sends your dominoes flipping head over heels into the next.

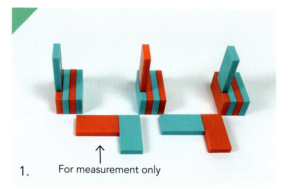

1. For measurement only

Place groups of four dominoes down with one vertical on the top left side. Space your stacks as shown above.

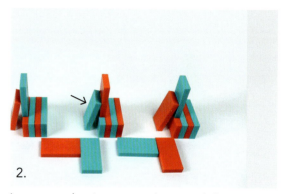

2.

Lean one domino on each vertical domino.

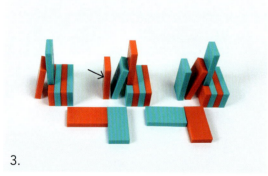

3.

Add one vertical domino next to the leaning dominoes.

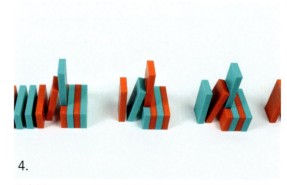

4.

Add horizontal lead-in line.

5.

Start the toppling and watch the dominoes go on a steam rolling rally.

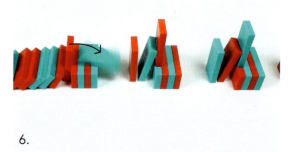

6.

This trick is awesome and sure to impress!

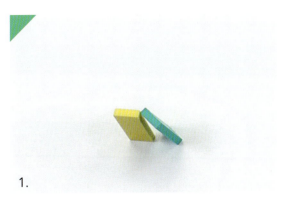

1.

Lean the upper corner of one domino into the next.

2.

Place the next domino in front of the leaning domino. Repeat the cycle a couple times.

As the dominoes fall in this trick they look as if they are falling backwards yet moving forwards.

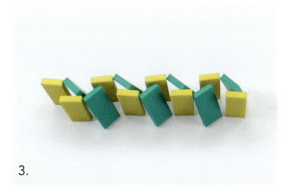

3.

Keep going as long as desired. Create lead-in and lead-out lines.

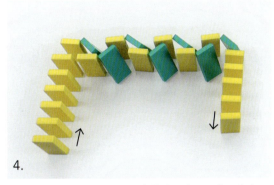

4.

Watch as it looks like it falls backwards while moving forwards.

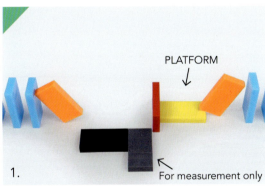

PLATFORM

1.

For measurement only

Carefully place the first leaning domino against a line. Leave a gap and create the platform for another leaning domino.

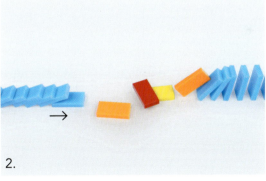

2.

The domino run will launch the leaning domino into the platform and cause the last to fall.

CANNON BALL

Throws a domino into a receiving platform. Allows gaps to be in your run.

THE STUN

A mystical trick as each domino seems to magically tip the next.

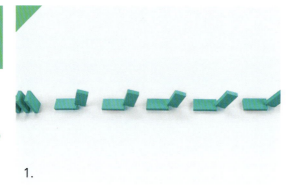

1.

Place leaning dominoes in a just-about-to-fall position on each flat domino.

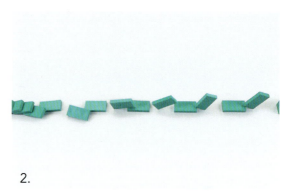

2.

As each domino falls it tips the next.

THE DOUBLE STUN

Easier than The Stun, but uses more dominoes to create the springing action.

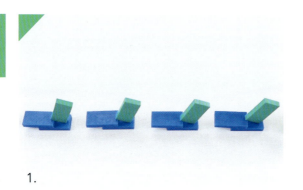

1.

Place two flat dominoes offset and then the leaning one on top of both.

2.

Watch as they tip and spring the rest of the dominoes off their platform.

ROUNDHOUSE KICK

This is exactly what it sounds like; dominoes roundhouse kicking the next. Set this up to give your dominoes some impressive moves.

1.

Build a lead-in line with four horizontal dominoes at the end.

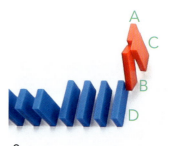

2.

Place one vertical domino a domino's length away(A). Lean a domino(B) between the horizontal(D) and vertical dominoes(C).

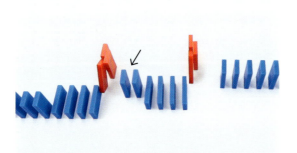

3.

Add another vertical domino slightly in front of the leaning domino. Repeat steps one through three.

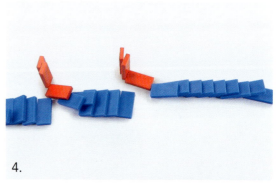

4.

Watch the dominoes spin and kick the next.

QUANTUM JUMP

Instantly transfer energy to another location with this trick. This is good for hiding transitions.

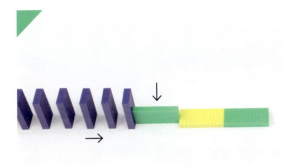

1.

Place one horizontal domino flush with a line of flat dominoes.

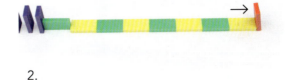

2.

Finish flat line and lean a domino against it at the end.

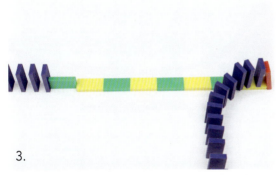

3.

Build the lead-out line on top of the flat dominoes, beginning at the leaning domino.

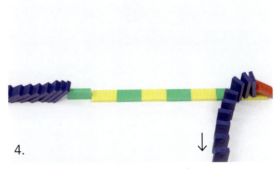

4.

Watch as the dominoes throw the energy through the flat dominoes instantly!

INSTANT TRANSFER

Instantly transfer your dominoes energy through this line and topple the next. This is capable of transferring longer distances than the Quantum Jump.

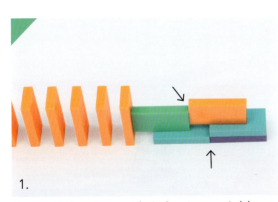

1.

Create 2-tier steps with 3 dominoes. Add two horizontal dominoes on top of the steps.

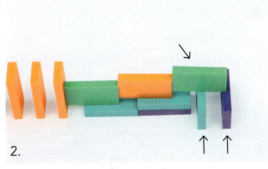

2.

Add on to the platform as shown in picture above.

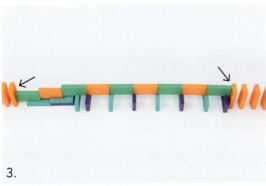

3.

Add to the platform until desired length is reached. Make sure lead-in and lead-out lines are touching the long horizontal line.

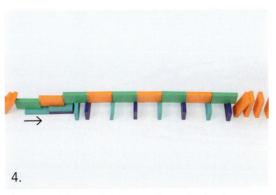

4.

The transition will happen in an instant.

ALTERNATOR

This trick will have dominoes falling in opposite directions in an alternating fashion.

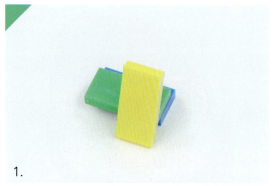

1.

Place two flat dominoes in a staircase fashion, with one vertical domino leaning against it.

2.

Repeat step one on the back side. Second staircase needs to be touching both vertical dominoes.

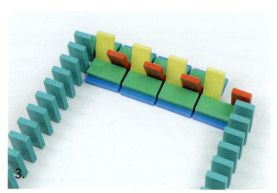

3.

Repeat steps one and two until desired length is reached.

4.

Add lead-in and lead-out lines.

DRAGON'S TEETH

This is an elaborate effect that causes a rippling effect along the structure.

1.

Create a staircase. Place five vertical, then three horizontal dominoes in a repeating pattern ending with a flat two domino stack.

2.

Begin placing dominoes as pictured above. Continue placing until all gaps are filled.

3.

Create a lead-in line with the last two dominoes placed horizontally. Place one vertical domino at the end to continue the run.

4.

Start the toppling and prepare for greatness!

1.

Place a domino flat, with another leaning halfway on top of it, and one vertical on top of the leaning domino.

2.

Repeat step one in a back and forth set up.

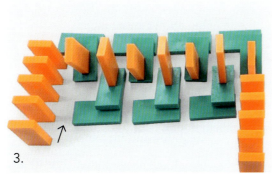

3.

Place your lead-in and lead-out lines.

4

Topple from the left and watch each domino slide and fall, triggering the next.

SLEEPERS

A tricky set up that slows down your run with an almost magical tipping effect.

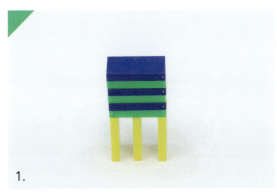

1.

Place three dominoes vertically then place a stack of six dominoes flat on top.

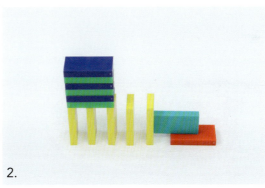

2.

Place two vertical dominoes after the stack, then place a flat domino with an offset horizontal domino, as shown above.

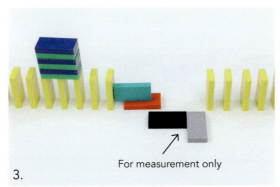

For measurement only

3.

Place a lead-in line, then space a lead-out line one and a half dominoes away from the launching domino.

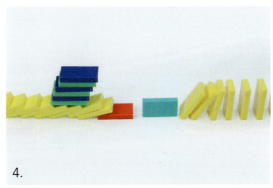

4.

Watch as the trick launches the domino forward.

STACKED LAUNCHER

The stack of dominoes will provide a lot of force to send the lead domino flying across the gap to continue the toppling. This method can be used in any situation that needs a little more force.

WAVE RIDER

The domino on top, quickly slides down into the next creating an up and down motion along the run.

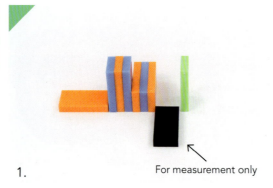

1.

For measurement only

Start setup as shown in the image above.

2.

Place dominoes as shown above. NOTE: horizontal domino should be almost falling off of the stack.

3.

Repeat steps one and two until desired length is reached.

4.

Prepare to be amazed as the dominoes ride the waves like a surfer.

HURDLE KICKS

This trick has dominoes kicking themselves into each other.

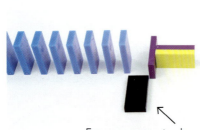

1.

For measurement only

Spacing is very important. Use a flat domino to measure the distance between the lead-in line and the platform.

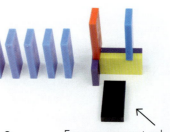

2.

For measurement only

Place two vertical dominoes on top of the platform.

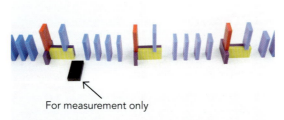

For measurement only

3.

Use at least four dominoes between each platform.

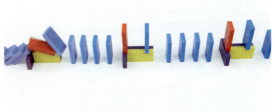

4.

Topple from left to right

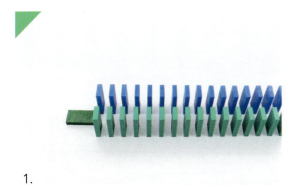

1.

Set up two lines that are close enough that dominoes can be placed on top to bridge the gap.

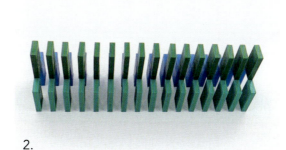

2.

Place dominoes vertically across the top.

POWER DIVE

This trick has dominoes falling off a ledge in one direction while leaving one line standing.

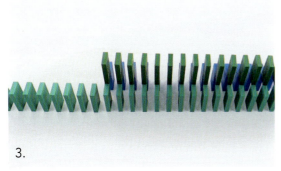

3.

Choose which side your lead-in line will topple.

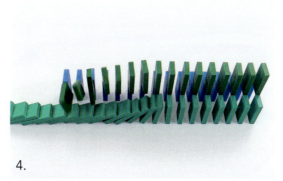

4.

Creates a neat diving effect.

1.

Setup dominoes as shown above. Take note of the offset after each diving domino.

2.

Add small line in front of offset domino.

SAILOR'S DIVE

In this trick, dominoes will dive off of the platforms into the next domino.

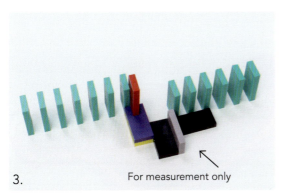

3.

For measurement only

Add a small line on the backside of the offset domino, take note of the spacing.

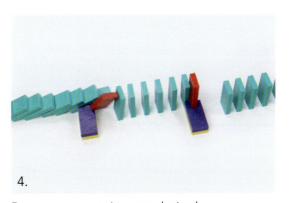

4.

Repeat as many times as desired.

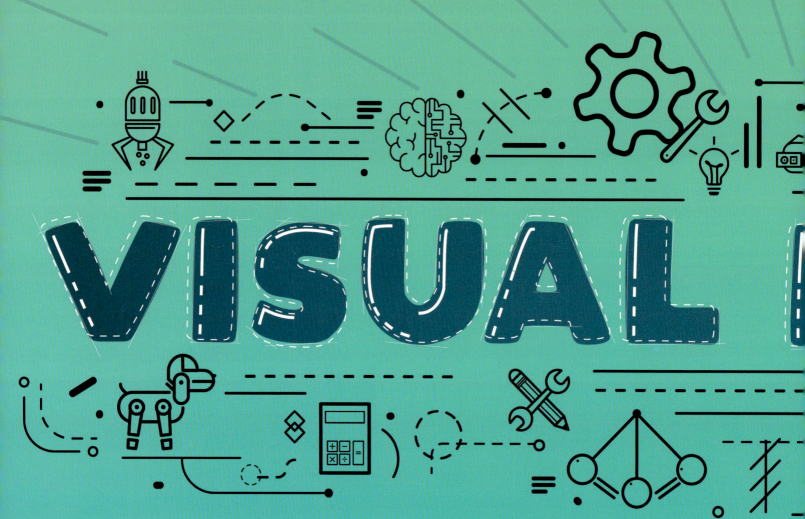

EFFECTS

Arrangements that display fascinating patterns during the toppling progression. These elaborate setups range from easy to difficult.

BERMUDA TRIANGLE

Dominoes will change directions as they fall, staggering and splaying out in a beautiful and intriguing pattern.

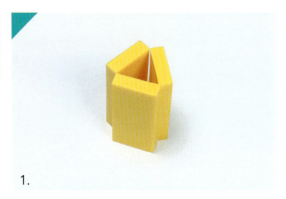

1.

Make a triangle using three dominoes. Have one of the three barely inside the other two.

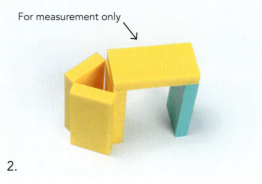

For measurement only

2.

Use a domino for the correct spacing to start the next triangle.

3.

Complete second triangle.

4.

Repeat previous steps, be sure to continue the trick from one of the dominoes that falls outwards.

5.

Complete third triangle.

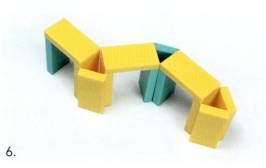

6.

If you want to continue the triangle in other directions, feel free. Two lines can be made from each triangle.

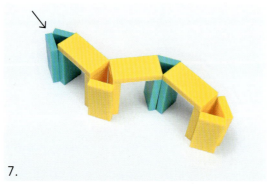

7.

Additional triangle setup in other direction.

8.

One more triangle...

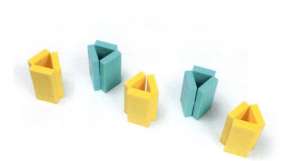

9.

Remove all "measurement only" dominoes.

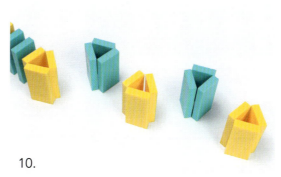

10.

Set up a lead-in domino line and it is ready to topple.

BOLSTERED BERMUDA TRIANGLE

The Bolstered Bermuda Triangle will topple a bit slower than the single dominoes but has more visual presence. Give it a try!

1.

Same setup as the regular Bermuda Triangle...

2.

Just add another domino on each side of the triangle.

3.

Use outside domino to measure distance from the next triangle and create a temporary bridge.

4.

Repeat previous steps.

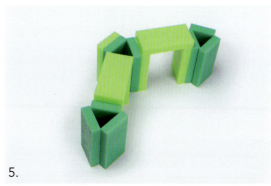

5.

Build in other directions from the triangles if needed, adding two dominoes to each side of the triangle.

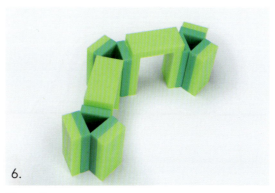

6.

Keep it up...

BOLSTERED BERMUDA TRIANGLE (CONT.)

7.

Build as many as you like until satisfied.

8.

Remove all "measurement only" dominoes.

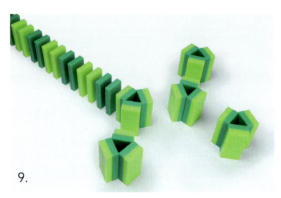

9.

Set up a lead-in domino line and it is ready to topple.

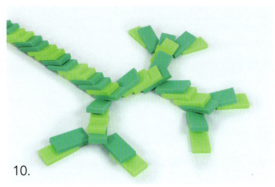

10.

End result is a multi-directional trick ready to amaze!

ZIPPER PULL

Easy and beautiful setup that will topple dominoes on each side of the run as it moves forward.

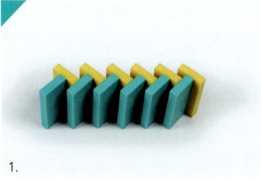

1.

Essentially, these are "T"s touching one another. Place all dominoes centered in each "T".

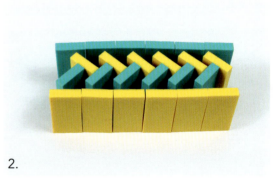

2.

Place a wall of dominoes on each side of Zipper Pull. This wall can serve as the beginning to a domino field.

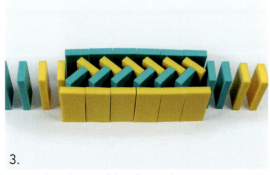

3.

Set up lead-in and lead-out dominoes.

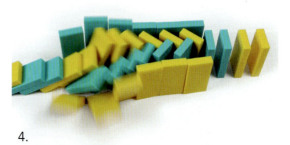

4.

Toppling from left to right, this is how it all goes down.

This setup will display hidden colors inside the box once toppled, kind of like fireworks. It's a nice unexpected surprise.

1.

Simple start..

2.

Make a "T" then place a domino that will be the toppling trigger.

3.

Place another domino off the top side of the "T", off-centered so that it fits neatly when boxed in.

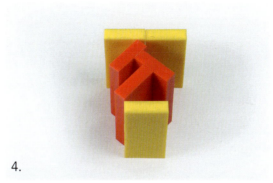

4.

Start creating your box, surrounding the middle red dominoes.

5.

Complete the box around the red dominoes.

6.

Create additional fireworks boxes off each side of the initial box.

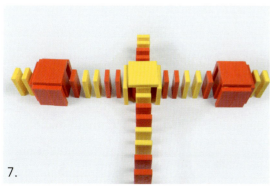

7.

Top each box with dominoes to hide the different colored dominoes in each box.

8.

Topple and watch the display unfold.

CASCADING WAVE

The Cascading Wave falls like an ocean wave. The wave will be more visible the longer it is.

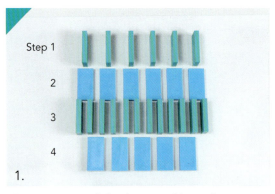

1.

This is an overall flat layout of how this setup will be built.

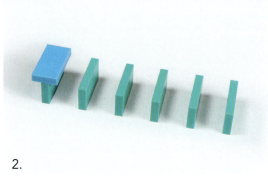

2.

Start placing flat dominoes on your bottom horizontal line, centered on each one.

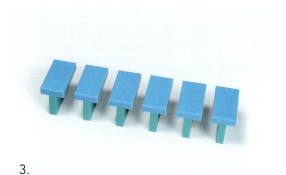

3.

Finish placing all flat dominoes.

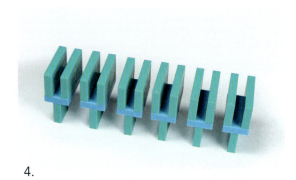

4.

Place two horizontal dominoes at the same time on each flat domino.

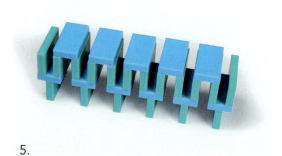

5.

Place flat dominoes on top, bridging the gap between each stack.

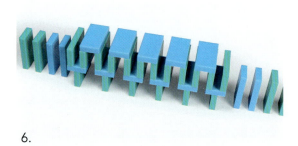

6.

Build your lead-in and lead-out lines...

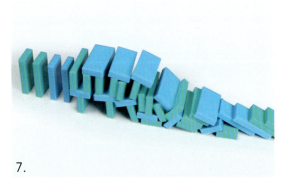

7.

Topple from either side and ride the wave!

8.

Build this trick as long as possible for even bigger waves.

1.

Begin a basic domino line then add two angled dominoes to create a Splitting Bolt.

2.

Build lines off the angled dominoes while creating additional Splitting Bolts.

3.

Repeat the process until satisfied.

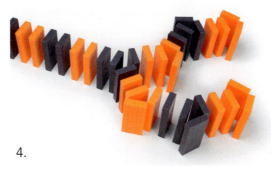

4.

Finish the starting domino line and it is complete.

SPLITTING BOLTS

Splitting Bolts are a simple way to make a basic line branch from left to right when toppling. This can also be used to add multiple lines branching off of one line.

1.

Start a horizontal domino line. Then begin staggering two at a time off the corner of the previous domino.

2.

Repeat in any direction you would like.

3.

Complete it by connecting it to another domino line to continue the chain reaction.

4.

The effect is a slow, left to right, crawling movement.

THE CATERPILLAR

This simple yet effective setup dances slowly from left to right in a crawly like movement.

DINO BONES

Dino Bones adds some interesting flare to an otherwise basic domino line. Its fast and its fancy.

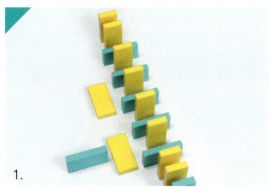

1.

Alternate one horizontal and one vertical domino until desired length. Horizontals should be less than one domino length apart.

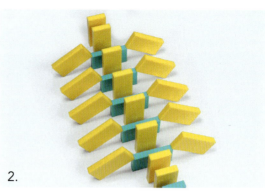

2.

Lean corners of dominoes on the corners of the horizontal dominoes, as shown above.

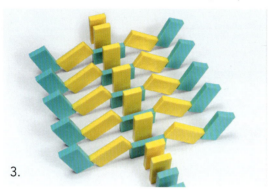

3.

Carefully place additional dominoes underneath the leaning dominoes so that it is leaning outward.

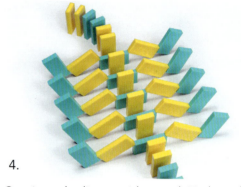

4.

Continue the line at either end. Trick works from either side.

THE GRAVITATOR

This trick will suddenly change the direction of your run in a sideways fashion. It will have your audience wondering how you actually did it.

1.

Line up a row of dominoes with a small gap between them. Then, place leaning dominoes at an angle against those dominoes.

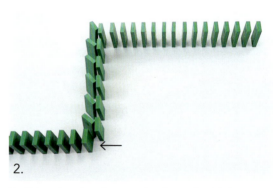

2.

Build a domino line on both ends. Make sure the line will hit the first t domino when toppled.

3.

Prepare to be "wowed!"

4.

This trick is a must learn!

HERRINGBONE

This is a very delicate setup but topples in a very unique way. It's worth the patience.

1.

Set up horizontal dominoes perpendicular to one another, lining them up like an "L" with a gap between them.

2.

Place a flat domino on top, bridging the gap, flush with the bottom dominoes with no overhang.

3.

Repeat step one and add another perpendicular domino on top of the first flat-laying domino.

4.

Place another domino on top. Repeat steps three and four until you reach the length of herringbone you desire.

5.

Stay consistent and be patient.

6.

You'll start to see a herringbone pattern.

7.

Build a lead-in line.

8.

They will fall in a staggered fashion and look awesome!

REVERSE WAVE

The bottom dominoes will topple forward while forcing the top dominoes to fall backwards.

1.

Set up a lead-in line, then a line of horizontal dominoes with vertical dominoes stacked on top.

2.

Leave one horizontal domino on each end unstacked. Looks like it is falling backwards while moving forwards.

DOUBLE REVERSE WAVE

This trick will also send dominoes flying backwards as your line moves forward.

1.

Set up two vertical dominoes and place one horizontal domino in between. Then, repeat this, leaving a gap between each group.

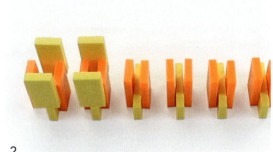

2.

Place vertical dominoes on each end of the horizontal dominoes.

3.

Create lead-in and lead-out lines.

4.

Topple left to right and watch the wave begin.

RUNNING TALL

Same as Reverse Wave except all dominoes are stacked vertically.

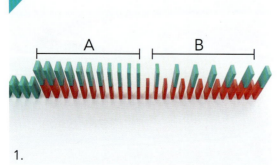

1.

Set up a lead-in line, then place vertical dominoes on top. Note the two different style options (A) and (B) in this setup.

2.

Falls similar to Reverse Wave and is great for big, loud topples.

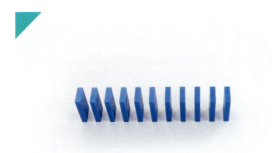

1.

Build a basic line.

2.

Stack vertical dominoes on the top and at the back of every two dominoes.

3.

Repeat step 2 but place them in the front alternating every two from the back. Then place verticals on the top connecting gaps.

4.

Add as many layers as desired. Build lead-in and lead-out lines. This trick creates big smiles.

DRAGON DANCE

1.

Make sure the dominoes on top are all in a straight line, as they need to hit each other when falling.

2.

Us a template for even spacing and easy setup.

Easy way to change orientation of dominoes and add some height to your run.

RIPPLE WAVE

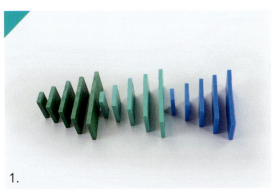

1.

You can make the waves as wide and long as desired.

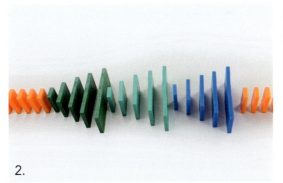

2.

Creates an interesting sound effect with flare.

Ripple Waves add visual variety, are easy to set up, and are a creative way to mix up your run.

KILTER RUN

As the dominoes topple it looks as if the leaning dominoes are leaping off the flat ones.

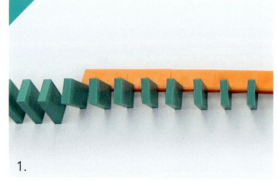

1.

Build a lead-in line, lay flat dominoes touching each other and place bottom corner of vertical dominoes on top of flat dominoes.

2.

Be sure to offset the flat dominoes from the lead-in line. Dominoes will fall sideways as they are tipping.

DOUBLE KILTER RUN

As the horizontal dominoes are toppled, they will topple the leaning lines on both sides and create a beautiful visual effect.

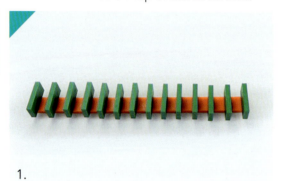

1.

Start out with dominoes flat at a length that is desired then place horizontal dominoes on top evenly spaced.

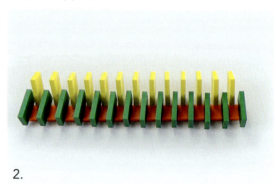

2.

Lean vertical dominoes between the horizontals, setting their bottom edge on the flat laying dominoes.

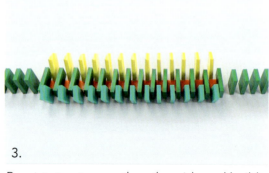

3.

Repeat step two on the other side and build lead-in and lead-out lines.

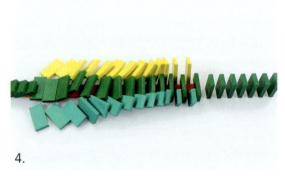

4.

Fans out on both sides as it topples.

STALACTITE

Just like in a cave, you can make these towers throughout your run for added visual effects.

1.

Build stalactite with 3 dominoes on the bottom, then 2, then 1. Create a separate run into each row of stalactites.

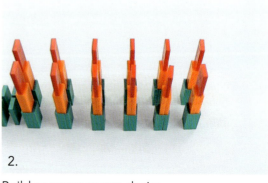

2.

Build as many as you desire.

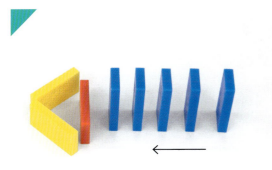

1.

Lay the first dominoes horizontal. Be sure to leave a small gap between the yellow and red dominoes.

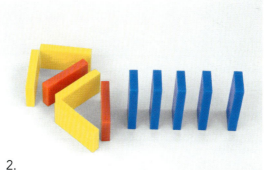

2.

Adding to the trick is simple. Just add another "slice" leading out from each of the yellow dominoes.

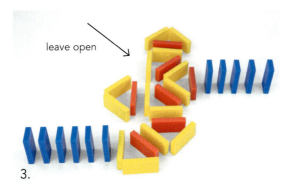

leave open

3.

Make as many "slices" as desired. Be sure you do not overcrowd when building.

4.

Are you hungry for a slice?

PIZZA SLICES

Pizza Slices creates a fantastic pattern when set up and a slow creative fall when it topples.

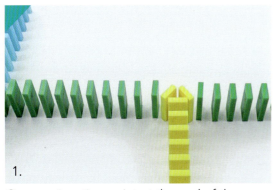

1.

Create a junction point at the end of the run with two 45° angled dominoes. Then split the run into two lines.

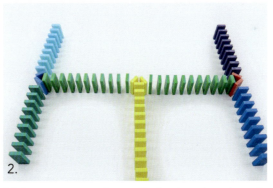

2.

Make as many splits as desired or that there is room for. Use the same amount of dominoes and spacing for each split.

SIMULTANEOUS DROP

This is a key method to timing multiple runs to fall at the same time.

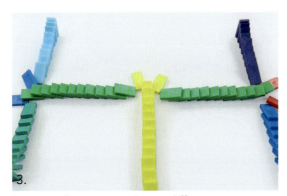

3.

It is good to use to trigger different runs at the same time.

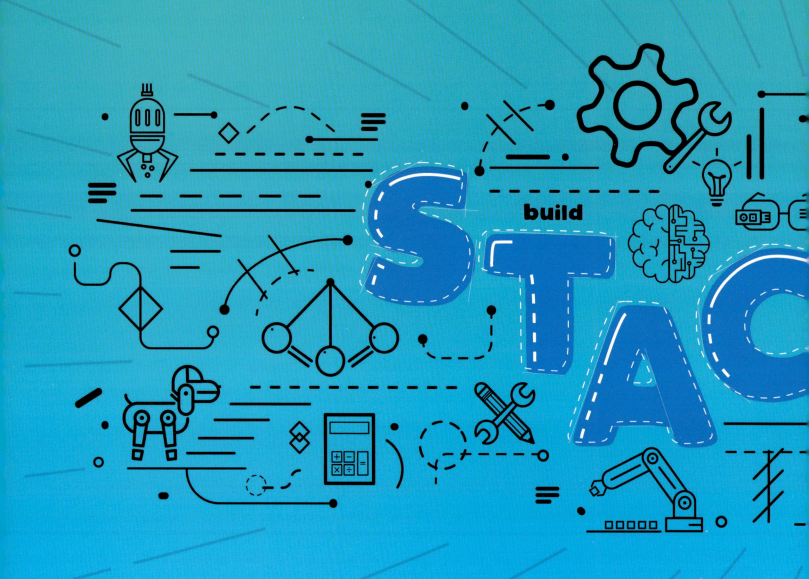

KING

assemble

Techniques that involve placing dominoes on top of one another to build walls, pyramids, towers, or vertical objects.

HORIZONTAL WALL

The Horizontal Wall can be any length or height you wish it to be. Scale it up or down according to your personal preference.

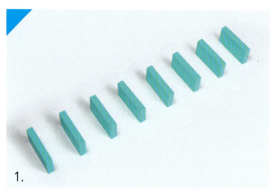

1. Start a single line of horizontal dominoes.

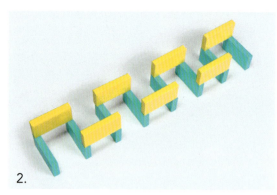

2. Stagger the next level of dominoes as seen above.

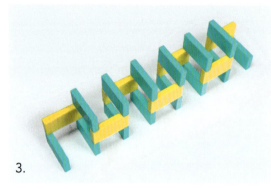

3. Add more horizontal dominoes to the tops of the last layer.

4. Add two vertical dominoes, one on each end of the bottom layer.

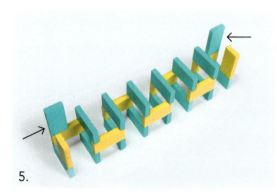

5. Add two more vertical dominoes, one on each end of the second layer.

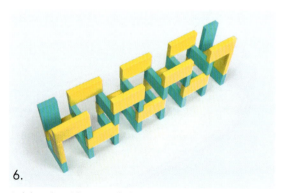

6. Add a third layer of dominoes with an alternate stagger as step two.

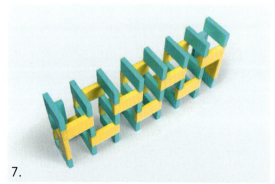

7. Add a fourth layer identical to step one.

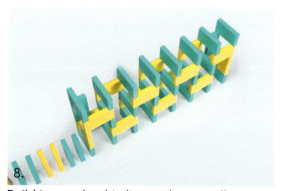

8. Build in your lead-in line and your wall is complete. Note: walls can be difficult to knock down.

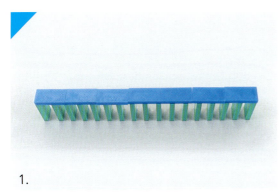

1.

Stack flat dominoes on top of a basic line. Make sure the dominoes line up at each end.

2.

Place a basic line on top of the flat dominoes.

DOUBLE TAKE

Watch your line climb the stairs, run the bridge, and come back around underneath the bridge to continue the run.

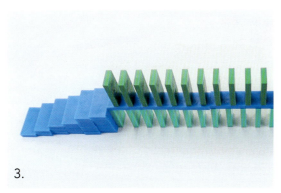

3.

Create a staircase lead-in, with seven dominoes in the highest stack.

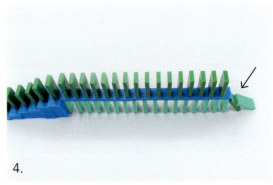

4.

Place a lead-in up the staircase. Add the leaning return dominoes at the end.

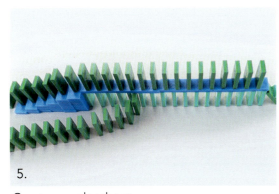

5.

Create your lead-out.

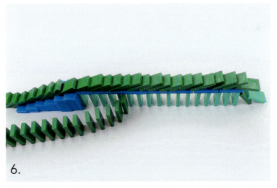

6.

This trick will topple across the top, fall and trigger the bottom row which will then trigger the lead-out line.

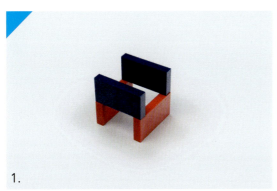

1.

Build by placing two alternating horizontal dominoes on top of each other.

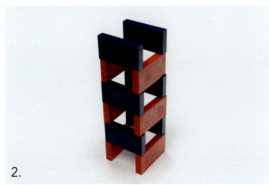

2.

These are extremely easy and fast to build and a great crowd pleaser!

BASIC TOWER

Super simple tower that can be made to any height. How high can you stack?

FALL WALL

The Fall Wall will create a cascade of dominoes when toppled, making a big pile at the bottom of the stack.

1.

Create a base of three vertical rows, make as long as desired.

2.

Add the next layer (two vertical rows), then one additional layer on top of that stack (one vertical row), creating a tall staircase.

3.

Stack the dominoes up the wall one layer at a time starting from the bottom. Place a lead-in line.

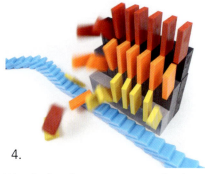

4.

Watch the dominoes cascade down the wall. Walls can be taller if you stack more rows behind the first three.

CRISSCROSS FALL WALL

A fall wall with a little more complexity.

1.

Create a base of flat dominoes, 3 high, 3 deep. Add layer two, 3 high, 2 deep. Add layer three, 3 high, 1 deep, creating stairs.

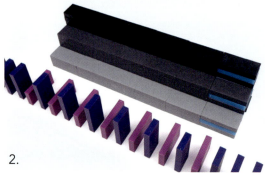

2.

Create a line, in an alternating vertical to horizontal pattern.

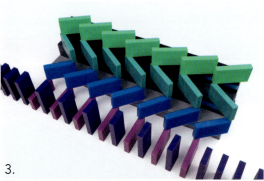

3.

Place dominoes up the wall at alternating 90° angles. Place a lead-in line. A lead-out line can be placed if desired.

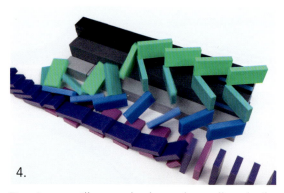

4.

Dominoes will cascade down the wall and pile at the bottom. It can be made in huge scale!

LIGHTNING WEAVE

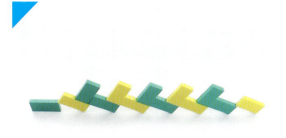

1.

Set up a lightning run and place the first layer of dominoes on top. Don't place a domino on the last section.

2.

Add the next layer. Make sure the line is straight.

Take a normal lightning run (pg. 19) and start stacking dominoes on top until you get an intricate weave pattern.

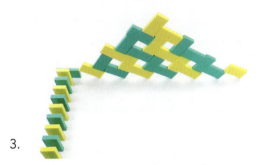

3.

Repeat the pattern up to the top. Create a lead-in line.

4.

Topples down easily. Has high spread of dominoes when falling.

LIGHTNING PYRAMID

1.

Create two lightning runs next to each other. Shorter than a dominoes distance apart.

2.

Add the second layer as shown above.

Add to the lightning weave and build 3D structures out of them. Easy to topple.

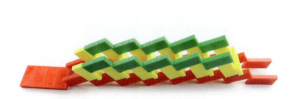

3.

Add the next layer.

4.

Repeat until you reach the top. Create a lead-in line and topple away.

WALL

This setup is easy and impressive at any scale.

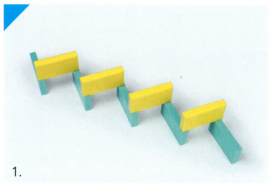

1.

Set the yellow dominoes perpendicular on top of the bottom dominoes, creating a visual zig zag with 90° angles.

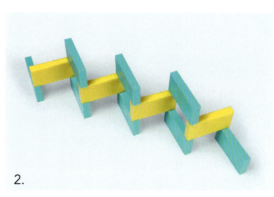

2.

Add the next layer. Be precise and make sure dominoes are parallel.

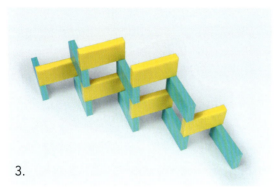

3.

Add the next layer.

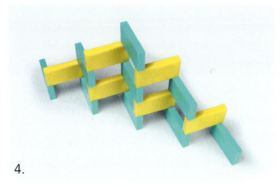

4.

Complete with one last domino. Can be expanded to greater heights and lengths.

SPEED PYRAMID

Easily toppled structure that is quick to build and is even faster to fall! A must learn.

1.

Build three basic stacks. Space each vertical domino the same distance apart.

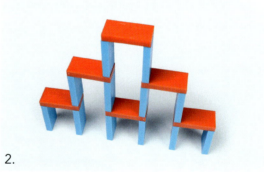

2.

Build two more stacks on top of the first layer, and one more on top of the second layer. Can be expanded to desired size.

SPEED WALL PYRAMID

By extending the speed pyramid, you can build speed walls!

1.

This trick is the same as the speed pyramid, just longer in length.

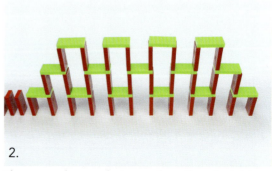

2.

These can be made to any length or height, and is sure to create huge smiles!

This exotic looking pyramid is sure to get attention.

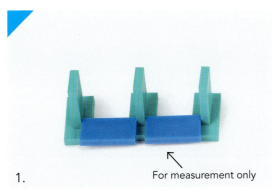

1.

For measurement only

Place three flat dominoes with vertical dominoes on top. You want the vertical dominoes one domino length apart.

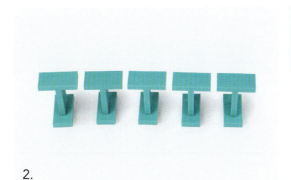

2.

Place flat dominoes on top of the vertical dominoes, exactly in the middle.

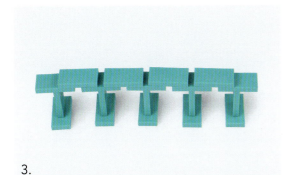

3.

Carefully place flat dominoes on top of step 2, bridging the gaps. Be as precise as possible.

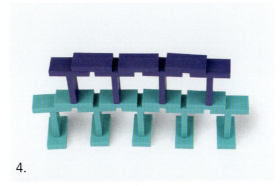

4.

Repeat steps 1, 2, and 3.

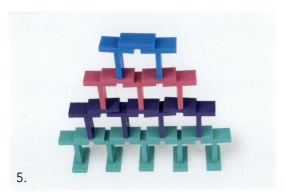

5.

Follow previous steps until you reach one stack on top.

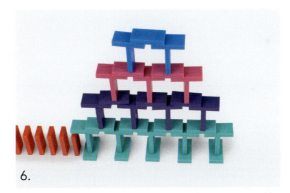

6.

Carefully build a lead-in line and pat yourself on the back.

PYRAMID WALL

Same as the Horizontal Wall but without the vertical dominoes on the end. Can be extended into a wall.

This trick can be made as large as you can imagine!

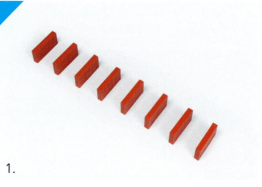

1.

Lay horizontal dominoes evenly spaced apart, at a distance where you are able to set one domino flush between the two.

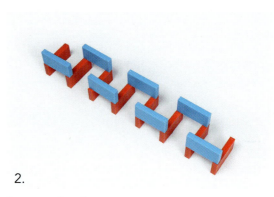

2.

Stagger the dominoes on top of the bottom layer.

3.

Make another straight row on top of the second layer.

4.

Repeat step 2 across the layer.

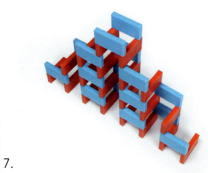

5.

Repeat step 3.

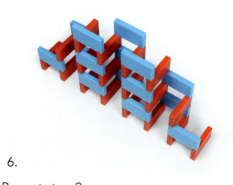

6.

Repeat step 2.

7.

Add the last dominoes on top of the final layers.

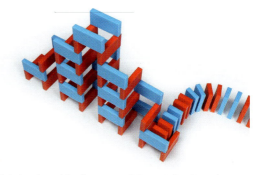

8.

Build the lead-in line on either side. Lead-in position is important, as it can require a lot of force to topple.

PYRAMID

Classic 3D structure that can be built to any size. Four sloping sides and a square base.

This is a 5x5 pyramid and it uses 95 dominoes. Can you make a 12x12?

1.

Set dominoes horizontal and parallel, less than the length of a domino apart.

2.

Set the next dominoes perpendicular on top of the bottom dominoes, creating a visual zig zag with 90° angles.

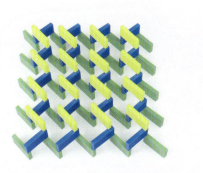

3.

Repeat step one on top of second layer. This uses fewer and fewer dominoes per layer.

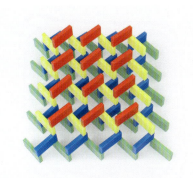

4.

Set additional perpendicular dominoes on top of the fourth layer.

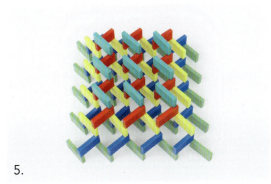

5.

Add the next layer...nine dominoes.

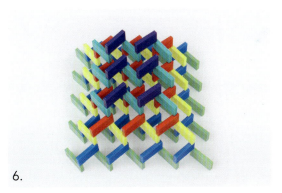

6.

Next layer... six dominoes.

7.

Next layer... four dominoes.

8.

Place the last two layers at the top. The Pyramid is now complete and it is epic!

WALL SPLITTER

This build is great for toppling two walls at the same time.

1.

Make a triangle from three dominoes with one domino slightly inside the other two.

2.

Set up two vertical dominoes on each side of the triangle. Set a horizontal domino on top of the triangle.

3.

Set one horizontal domino on top of the two vertical ones on each side.

4.

Two more dominoes get placed on top, bridging the gaps.

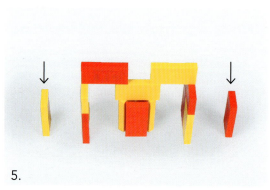

5.

Place two dominoes vertically on the outside.

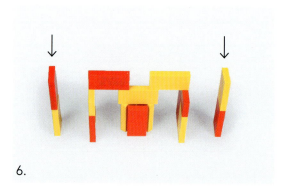

6.

Place another on top of the vertical dominoes on each side.

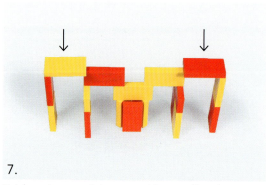

7.

Bridge the outside gap with one flat domino on each side.

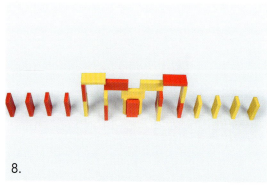

8.

Set up four vertical dominoes on each side, less than one domino length apart.

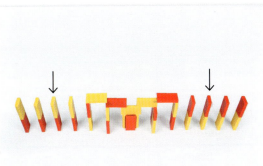

9.

Set another four vertical dominoes on top of the ones just placed in last step.

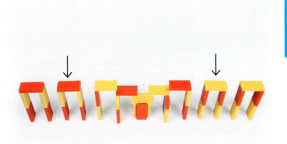

10.

Add flat dominoes to the vertically stacked dominoes, making mini towers.

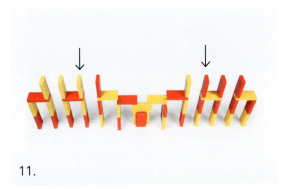

11.

Add vertical dominoes on the top of each tower.

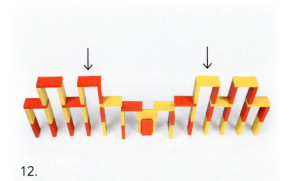

12.

Add flat dominoes to the tops of the mini towers.

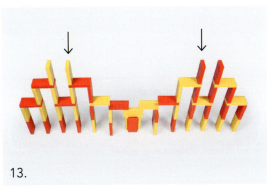

13.

Add vertical dominoes to create the last tier of the towers.

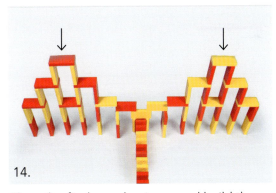

14.

Place the final two dominoes and build the lead-in line out from the middle triangle.

RAZOR BACK PYRAMID

The Razor Back Pyramid is easy to build, looks cool, and topples backwards.

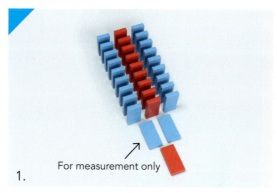

1.

For measurement only

Line up three lines of dominoes to create a small field.

2.

Add two lines of dominoes stacked on top of the bottom layer.

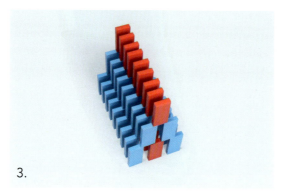

3.

Add last layer of dominoes in between and on top of the second layer.

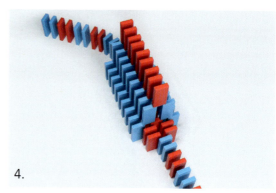

4.

Add a lead-in and lead-out line in order to continue after the pyramid topples.

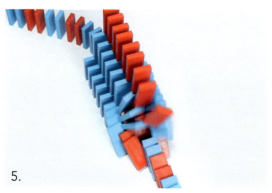

5.

Pyramid toppling backwards as it continues forward.

6.

Crowd cheers!

CASTLE

Have you ever wanted to see a castle get destroyed? Now you can!

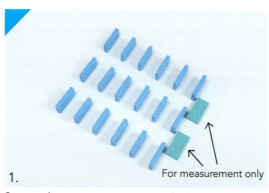

1.

For measurement only

Space dominoes as measured above.

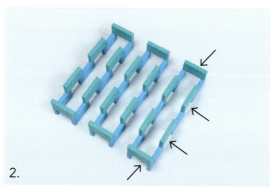

2.

Stack dominoes on the ends and through the middle.

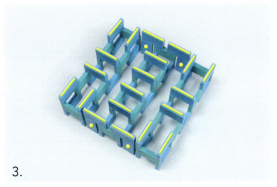

3.

Yellow lines indicate the next layer of stacked dominoes. Yellow dots indicate vertical dominoes.

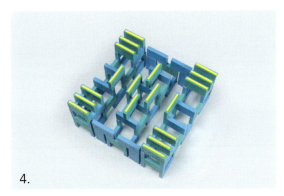

4.

Continue the next layer...

CASTLE (CONT.)

Looks can be deceiving. This castle is easy to build, very stable, and will visually enhance your setup.

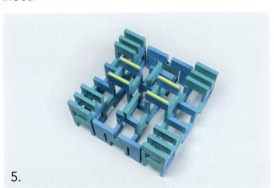

5.

Start building up the center...

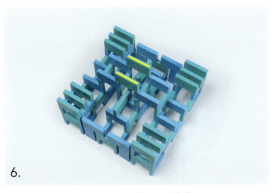

6.

Add the base layer for the middle tower.

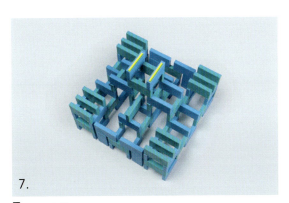

7.

Two more...

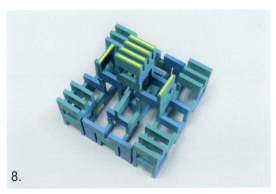

8.

Add four at the top and the castle structure is now complete.

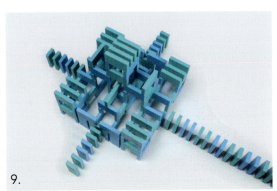

9.

Build lead-in and lead-out lines in any or all directions from each side hitting the middle domino.

10.

Enjoy the destruction! It was a beautiful castle...

TOWER TUMBLE

A great method to knock down sturdy towers.

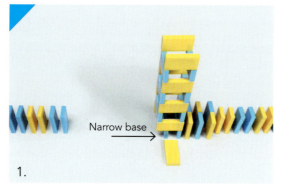

1.

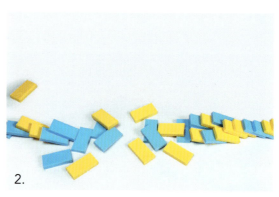

2.

Build a basic tower with a narrow base. Build a lead-in line using a few rows of two dominoes side by side.

The tower will topple all at once.

TOWER SIEGE

Another method to knock down sturdy towers.

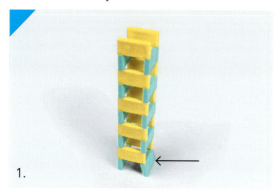

1.

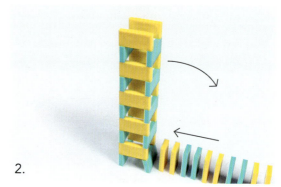

2.

Build a basic tower. Once built, tilt one of the bottom dominoes out while holding the other steady. Be careful.

Build a lead-in line to hit the tilted domino and it will fall backwards all at once.

THE WATERFALL

A tower that, when triggered, progressively dumps dominoes and crumbles while standing.

1.

2.

Stack the dominoes so they are all flat on the back side of the tower.

Continue pattern until the desired height. Start the reaction by tipping the second topmost domino down.

3.

4.

Dominoes will fall one by one in a pile off the tower. . .

This trick is incredibly satisfying to watch!

Topple it for a big effect! The cube can be scaled to any size.

1.

First layer. Keep dominoes perfectly parallel and evenly spaced, a domino's length apart.

2.

Second layer.

3.

Third layer.

4.

Fourth layer.

5.

Fifth layer.

6.

Sixth layer.

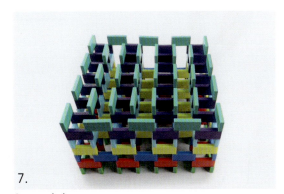

7.

Seventh layer.

8.

Eighth layer, keep adding layers until the height is the same length as the sides. Cubes are real show stoppers!

IMPLODING TOWER

The Imploding Tower looks odd at first but you'll quickly see the pattern and watch it topple from inside out, top to bottom.

1.

Starting point...

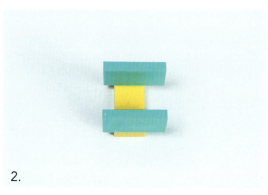

2.

Make sure dominoes are flush with the ends of the bottom domino.

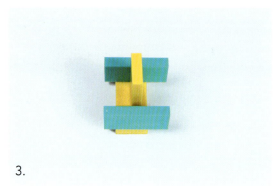

3.

Add one vertical domino standing in the middle on the right half on the bottom domino.

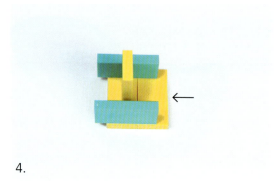

4.

Add another base domino.

5.

Add a horizontal domino between the two.

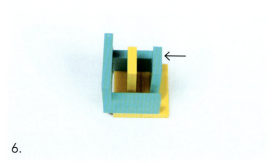

6.

Add an additional vertical domino on the left half of the right base domino.

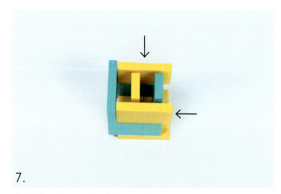

7.

Add horizontal side walls.

8.

Add flat domino flush with the edge of the left inside vertical domino.

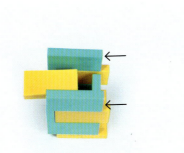

9

Add side wall dominoes.

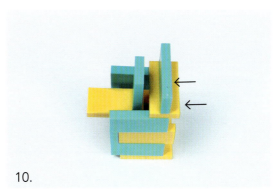

10.

Add a vertical domino in the middle. Add a flat domino while placing the horizontal upright domino on top.

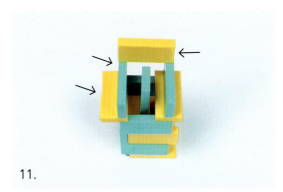

11.

Add a flat and horizontal domino on the left side, then add a horizontal domino perpendicular on top, across the gap.

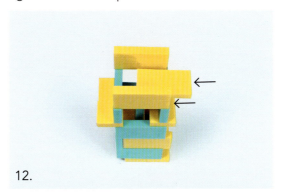

12.

Add an additional side wall and flat domino flush with the vertical middle domino.

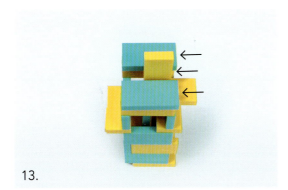

13.

Add one vertical domino on top of the middle flat domino. Add two flat dominoes centered with the side wall dominoes.

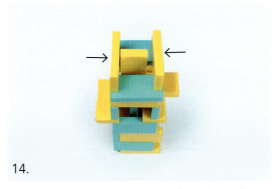

14.

Lay two dominoes horizontal for side walls. Move inside vertical domino to touch left wall flush.

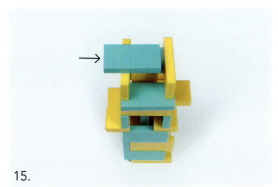

15.

Add a flat domino on top of the middle vertical domino and left side wall.

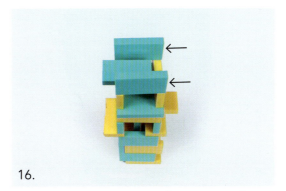

16.

Place two more side walls, front and back.

IMPLODING TOWER (CONT.)

This is an intricate tower that causes the tower to fall apart where it stands, instead of tipping over.

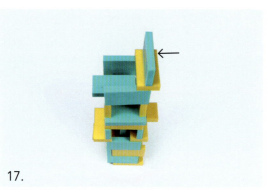

17.
Add a flat domino while at the same time placing a horizontal one on top.

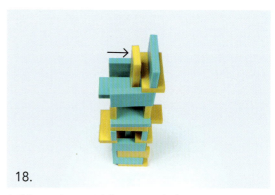

18.
Add another middle vertical domino.

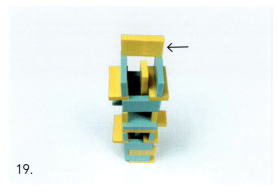

19.
Repeat step 17 on left side and add horizontal domino on back.

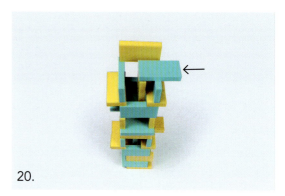

20.
Add a flat domino across the middle domino and right side wall.

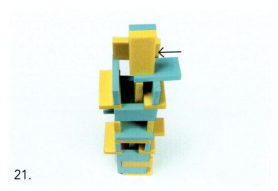

21.
Add two vertical dominoes on the edge of the flat domino and middle piece.

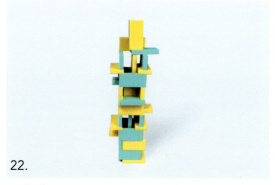

22.
Imploding Tower is now complete and ready for it's lead-in line to be built..

23.
View of what the tower should look like from left side.

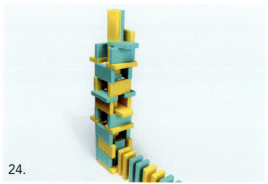

24.
View of tower from right side with lead-in line. Ready to topple.

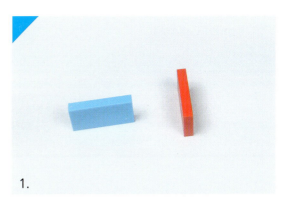

1.

Space dominoes just under the length of a domino.

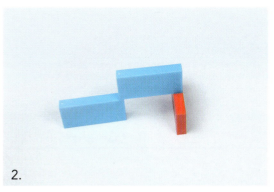

2.

Add a domino on top of the two, flush with the edge of the perpendicular domino.

LIGHTNING TOWER

Lightning run that travels up in a staircase fashion and can be lengthened to greater heights.

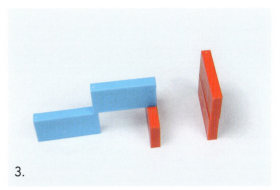

3.

Add two stacked horizontal dominoes.

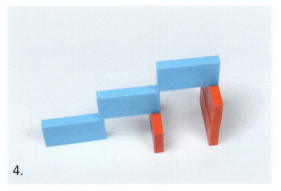

4.

Add another tier.

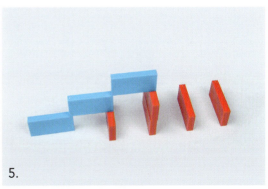

5.

Add two dominoes spaced at the same distance as the rest of the build.

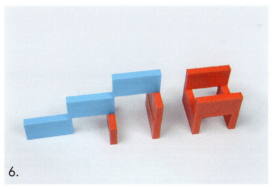

6.

Add two more perpendicular dominoes to build a mini tower.

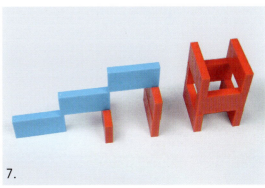

7.

Add two more perpendicular on the mini tower.

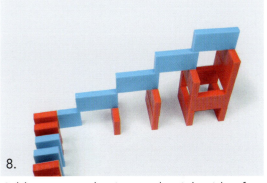

8.

Add one more domino on the right side of the tower and complete the build with two additional dominoes and a lead-in line.

SPIRAL SPEED WALL

A speed wall effect that forms a spiraling tower. Once learned, this trick can be expanded to varying sizes.

1.

Start with two vertical dominoes.

2.

Top them with a flat domino.

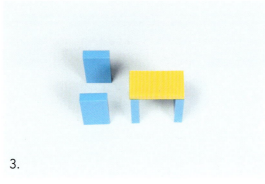

3.

Add two more vertical dominoes.

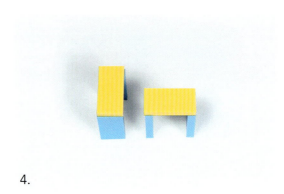

4.

Top it with a flat domino.

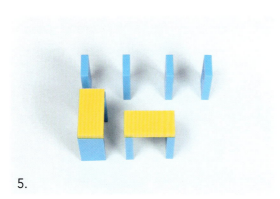

5.

Add four vertical dominoes spaced evenly apart.

6.

Top them with two flat dominoes.

7.

Continue process, going around the outside of each build.

8.

Repeat process.

9.

Repeat step five on the opposite side.

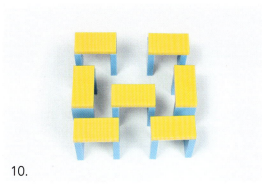

10.

Top them with flat dominoes.

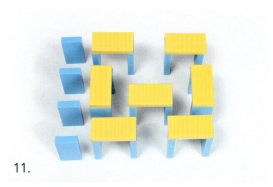

11.

Repeat step three on the outside of your build.

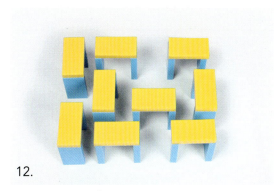

12.

Top them with flat dominoes.

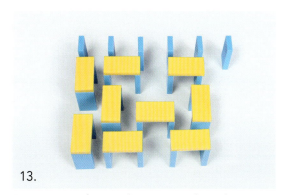

13.

Repeat step five, with six vertical on the outside.

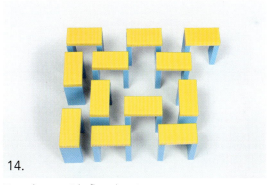

14.

Top them with flat dominoes.

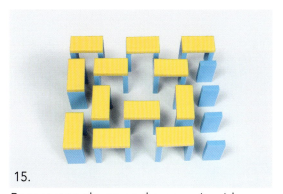

15.

Repeat step eleven on the opposite side.

16.

Top them with flat dominoes.

SPIRAL SPEED WALL (CONT.)

This trick will stun all who watch with it's mesmerizing implosion.

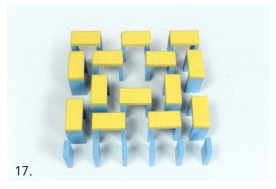

17.

Repeat step thirteen on the opposite side.

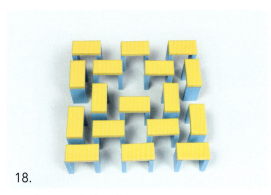

18.

Top them with flat dominoes.

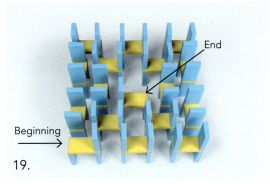

19.

Except for the beginning and end, add vertical dominoes on top of the stacks, above the vertical dominoes in the bottom row.

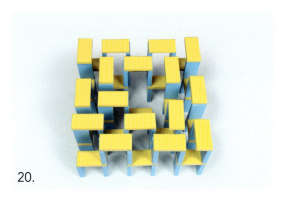

20.

Top all the vertical dominoes, bridging the gap between the stacks on the bottom.

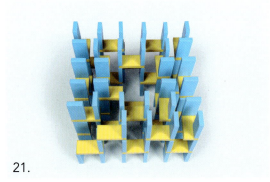

21.

Repeat step nineteen for an additional layer.

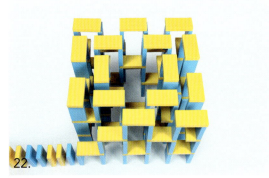

22.

Top them all with flat dominoes, build a lead-in line, and your ready for a toppling extravaganza!

KNOCKOUT TOWER

A tower that will collapse only down the center leaving the two sides standing.

1.

Set four parallel horizontal dominoes connected by three horizontal dominoes on top, as shown above.

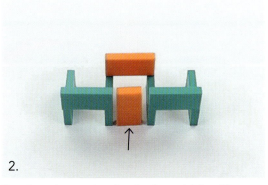

2.

Set the trigger domino in the middle. The lead-in line will topple this domino.

KNOCKOUT TOWER (CONT.)

You can knock down the two remaining towers in your run if you prefer to not leave anything standing.

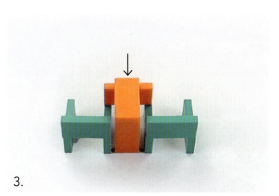

3.

Bridge the gap.

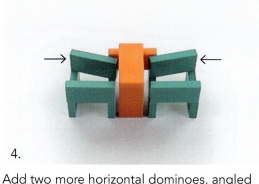

4.

Add two more horizontal dominoes, angled inward.

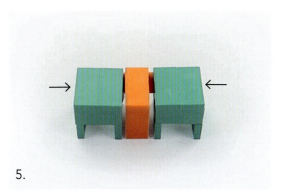

5.

Place flat dominoes over the gaps.

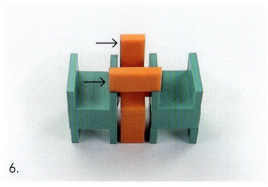

6.

Start the next layer but flip the center domino locations.

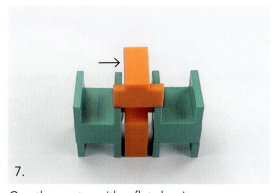

7.

Cap the center with a flat domino.

8.

Finish the layer and keep adding layers. The center dominoes will alternate back and forth.

9.

Add a lead-in line. The tower can be as tall as you want.

10.

Only the center of the tower will fall. Leaving the rest of the tower to be toppled later.

BATTERING RAM

Use this method to knock down sturdy walls and towers.

1.

Build a basic tower.

2.

Pull the bottom corner domino out from the bottom of the tower. Add a flat domino next to the corner with a horizontal one on top.

3.

Follow instructions for the Stack Launcher (pg. 65) to complete the Battering Ram.

4.

Watch it crumble.

THE STACK

This is a balancing act and a challenge! How many can you stack?

1.

Stand one domino up vertically. Lay one flat domino on top. Then two perpendicularly. Then three and so on.

2.

Balance as many as possible before it topples. These can be integrated into runs.

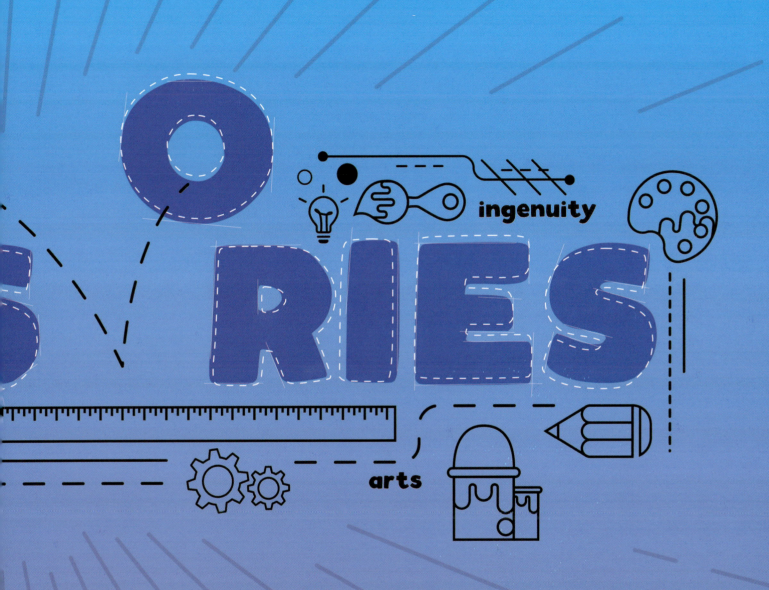

ingenuity

arts

Objects other than dominoes that are used to change directions, complete chain reactions, bridge gaps, increase or decrease elevation, or add an interesting twist to the overall setup.

SPINNERS

180°

Change the direction of your run! Great for tight locations.

1.

The run will quickly change direction.

2.

Keep the lines of dominoes relatively close to the spinner paddle.

180° MAINTAINED

Spinners can be added into any run that has already been placed.

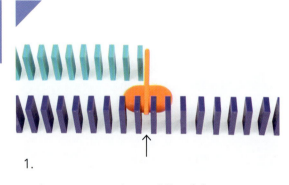

1.

Put the spinner in the middle of the run.

2.

Place the lead-out line. This creates a unique split in the run.

180° HAND-OFF MAINTAINED

Remove the paddle of the spinner to make a safety stop.

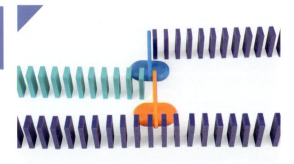

1.

Insert the spinner into a run. Place the next spinner on the back-hand side of the paddle.

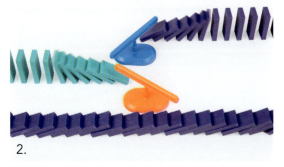

2.

Place lead-out lines at each toppling joint of the spinners.

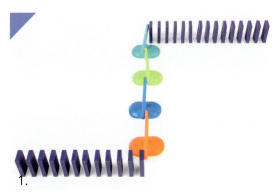

1.

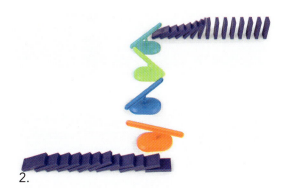

2.

Move in perpendicular motions with a line of spinners.

Place an even number of spinners to hand off the run in the same direction.

This is a good trick if you need to rapidly move a run or just show off.

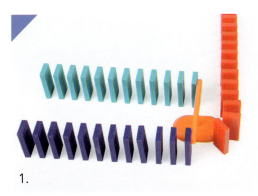

1.

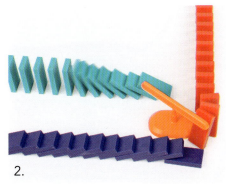

2.

ROUND ABOUT

Don't be afraid to try something new.

Set the line going around the corner a short distance away while placing the reversing run up against the paddle.

Mid action shot.

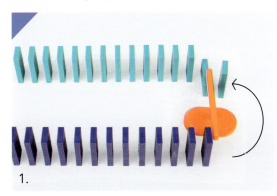

1.

2.

HALF SPIN

Insert a domino in the base of the spinner to help it not slide around.

Set a lead-in line. On the other side, place a horizontal domino under the paddle with a vertical domino in front of paddle.

The lead-out line should not be in the path of the paddle. The spinner will spin a half turn and knock down that front domino.

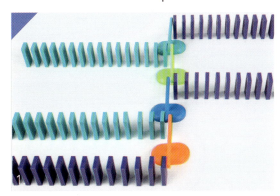

1.

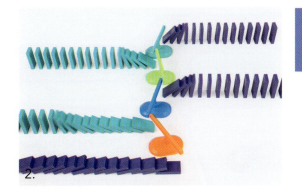

2.

ALL IN

This trick creates a split of 4 runs from one reaction.

When placing the spinners, make sure each paddle is up against the next and that each run is close to the spinner paddles.

Watch as the spinners all move at once knocking down all the dominoes.

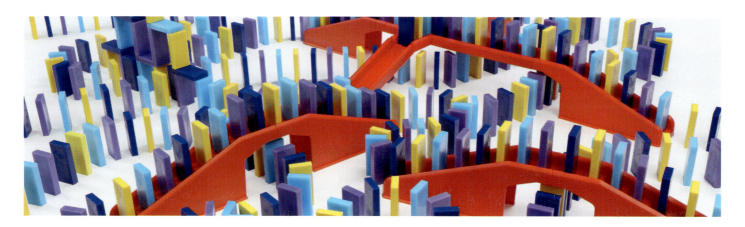

BRIDGES

SINGLE BRIDGE

Bridges are an easy way to go over a run that has been placed already.

1.

Take two bridge sections and connect them together.

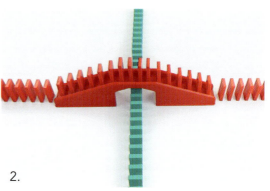

2.

Place bridge over run and place dominoes on it.

BRIDGE WITH STRAIGHT TRACK

Straight track can extend the bridge's length in case you need to go over multiple lines.

1.

Take one bridge and a straight track and connect them together.

2.

Place them over runs that you want to bridge. Place dominoes over bridge.

BRIDGES WITH 4-WAY SPLITTER

4-ways allow your bridges to change direction at 90° angles.

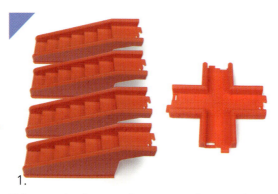

1.

Take two bridges and a 4-way splitter and connect them together.

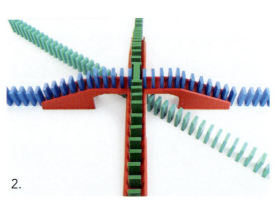

2.

You can use a crossover trick in the middle of the 4-way splitter to use both directions.

ARCS

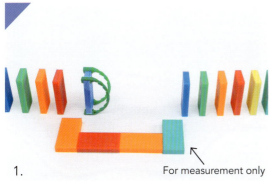

1.

For measurement only

Attach two Arcs onto the same side of a domino. Use dominoes to measure the distance (as seen above).

2.

Watch the domino roll, flip, and then flop right into the next run.

FLIPPING ARCS

Arcs can be attached to dominoes in a variety of ways.

1.

Attach two Arcs on both sides of the horizontal dominoes (or planks), (2 on each side).

2.

Create a lead-in and a lead-out a short distance away. Topple and watch the dominoes roll away.

ROLLING ARCS

Test rolling Arcs to see how far they will roll before putting them in your run. Can you get them to roll across the floor?

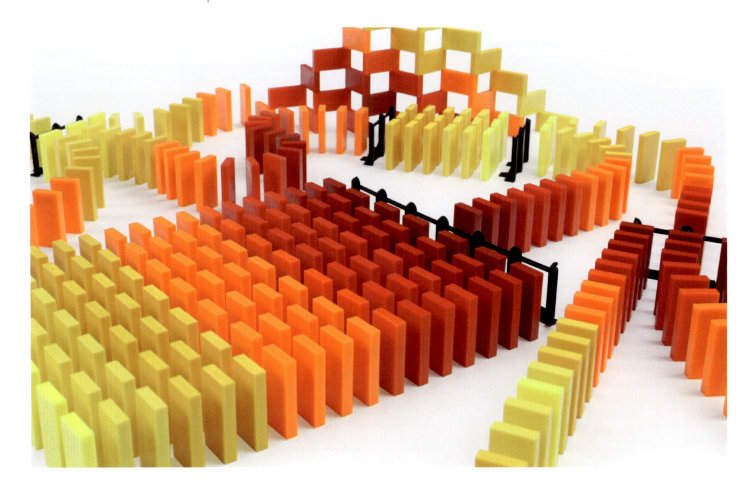

LINE REACTOR

THE SINGLE

These make transitions easy when you need to go from one run to multiple runs all at once.

1.
Single Line Reactor.

2.
Run one line into the reactor and then place up to three runs after it to split your runs easily.

THE DOUBLE

They link to themselves allowing them to extend to greater widths for massive knock down power.

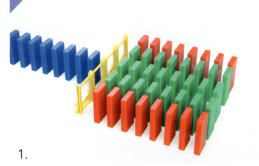

1.
One line of dominoes will knock down multiple connected Line Reactors.

2.
This will knock down many lines of dominoes at once!

TEMPLATE

RACK 'EM UP

Stack dominoes with ease by using a template. They make adding to runs hassle free and ensure dominoes are set up in a straight line. Vital for any large field set up. Great for kids and those that have a difficult time setting up dominoes. It makes it easy!

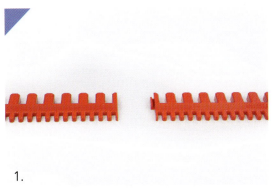

1.

Each template has a clip on the end which allows for multiple templates to be utilized at once.

2.

Clip them together to extend how many dominoes that can be set up simultaneously.

3.

Place the dominoes in the slots of the template.

4.

Push the template slightly forward and then carefully pull the template back.

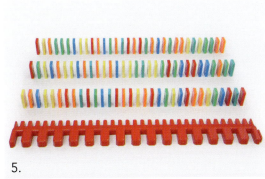

5.

Flip the template around and it will work with Mini Dominoes as well.

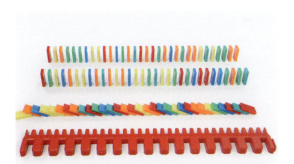

6.

Rack them up and then topple.

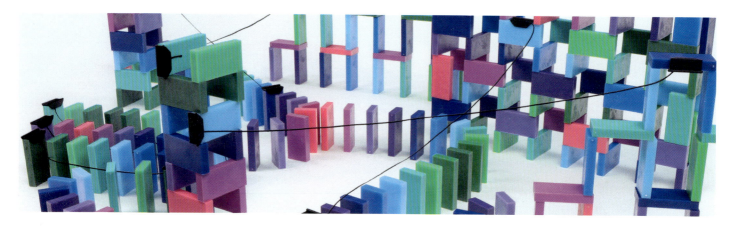

CLIPS 'N' STRING

TOP 'N' DROP

Create almost "magical" reactions by using strings and clips. This is a great way to transfer the energy up to a different level or height without having to build an elaborate staircase or tower.

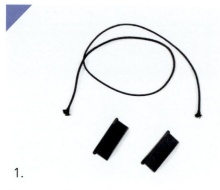

1.

Take two clips and a piece of string.

2.

Connect the dominoes together by clipping the string onto the domino.

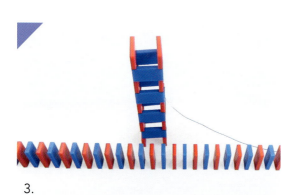

3.

Take down tough towers and walls with this method.

4.

It is easier to pull down dominoes that are higher in the tower. But be sure it is far enough down that the tower will topple.

RIPCORD

Transport your run from one location to another with this awesome trick!

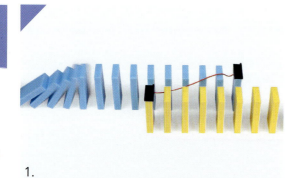

1.

If you use "invisible" string it will make your dominoes look like they are magically tipping over.

2.

Make sure that the first clipped domino falls in the correct direction to topple your run correctly.

BD 5000 LAUNCHER

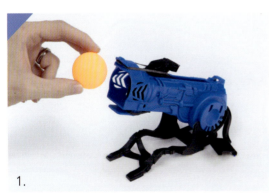

1.
Pick an angle to launch from and insert the ping pong ball.

2.
Pull back and lock and the launcher is now ready.

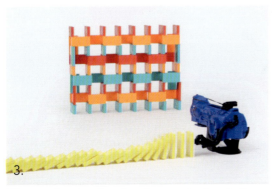

3.
Place a domino line leading up to the Activation Switch.

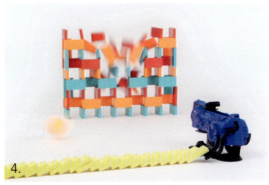

4.
Trip the Activation Switch to launch the ping pong ball into your structures.

LOCK 'N' LOAD

The launcher is the ultimate accessory! Powered by elasticity, the BD 5000 is ready to add fun to any chain reaction or domino run. Now you can REALLY let 'em fly!

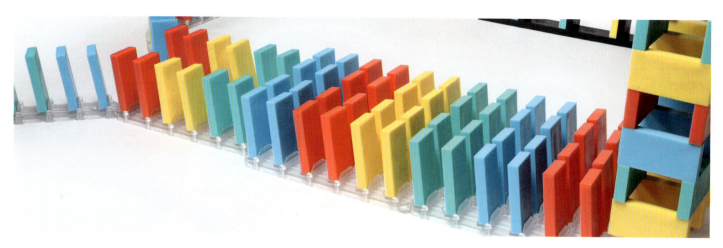

RAPID TRACK

Set up dominoes in an instant and with ease. Great for young builders and uneven surfaces. With Rapid Track, your runs can quickly and easily reset again and again and again!

1.

Rapid Track makes it so anyone can set up amazing domino runs!

2.

This is the rate at which rapid track can climb and still topple. To bridge other dominoes, you need to be about 8 dominoes high.

3.

Track segments can hook together aiding in their placement. A turn in the track is set for about 45°.

4.

Another example of how the track can be laid out. There are lots of options.

5.

Kinetic Planks, Electro Dominoes, Clear Dominoes, Kinetic Dominoes, and Pro Dominoes are all compatible with Rapid Track.

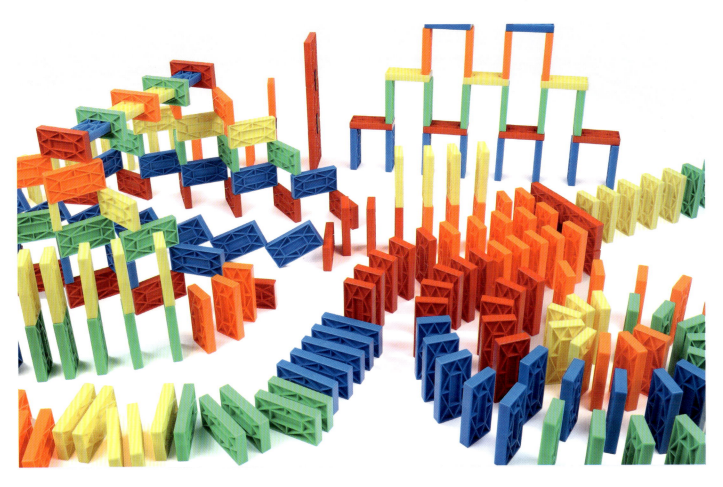

XL DOMINOES

1.

Clip blocks together to form larger dominoes so that they topple smallest to largest.

2.

Continue clipping blocks together until desired height is achieved.

GRADUATED BLOCKS

Clip blocks together to form giant dominoes and topple any structure that gets in their way!

3.

These can be made to any size. Note: Pro Dominoes are leading up to the first Geomni-block.

4.

Example: these are a sure way to topple large 3D setups.

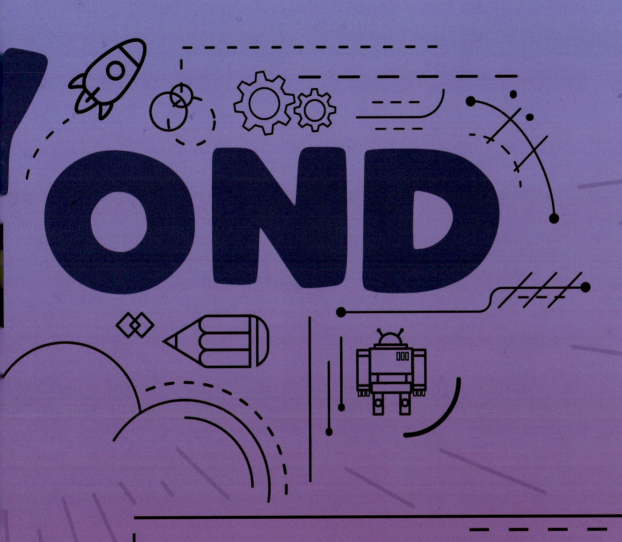

OND

Learn how to create beautiful domino vidoes, set records, start your very own domino club, and so much more!

Creating Domino Videos

Domino videos have thrilled and amazed millions with the fast speed and mesmerizing sounds of hours of hard work falling to the ground. Who doesn't like watching dominoes fall? The energy and excitement is contagious! Use the technology that is so readily available, capture the thrill of dominoes toppling and share it for others to see. Some have taken it to a professional level and post amazing domino setups online for the world to watch. What started as a hobby and love of toppling has led to many domino topplers traveling the world, making large setups for events, movies, TV commercials, and organizational gatherings.

We want to offer some tips on capturing dominoes on video that will help make setups look more professional.

For videos in general:

• Have a uniform background or have a theme to the background. This will help viewers to not be distracted while watching the dominoes topple. Make sure the environment is cleaned up and looks neat.
• Use color themes so the dominoes will look good on screen.
• Have good lighting if possible. Light goes a long way in helping video cameras capture a good looking video.

Before starting a video it is a good idea to decide what style of video to do. There are a few different styles that we want to mention:

Screen-link Videos

This style of video involves a domino setup that starts in frame and then runs out of frame. The view changes showing the last "line" running into the new frame and then eventually out of frame. This process is repeated until the last view shows the domino run ending. All of these video segments are then edited together to form one continuous run that goes from one view to the next.

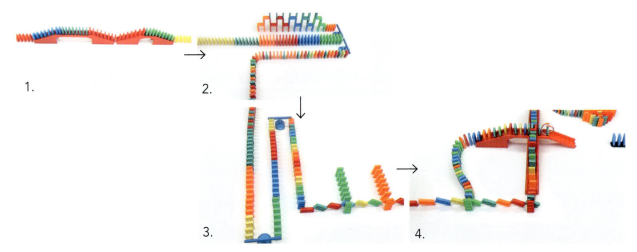

1.   2.

3.   4.

An advantage with using this method, is that it utilizes several small setups, that appear to be one continuous large setup, without the labor and risk of building a large continuous setup. Screen-links make it easier for builders who have smaller space and fewer dominoes to make that epic video of their domino building dreams!

 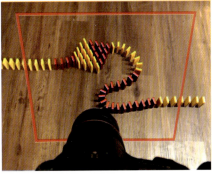 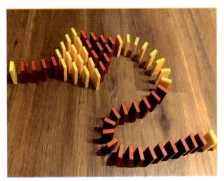

For seamless audio transitions from one screen-link to the next, it is important to setup extra dominoes outside the cameras live view area so that you have a consistent speed of dominoes falling through the video transitions. When the next frame starts the dominoes will be up to the same speed before entering the frame. It is also important to hold the same camera angle for each screen-link. We recommend a tripod. Lastly, to make the domino run transitions smoother, coordinate and place the run lead-in and run lead-out correctly from frame to frame, so that it makes sense on screen.

Following the Run Videos

In these videos, the camera follows the dominoes that are toppling for some close up action shots. There are a few things to note for these videos. On large setups, following the action of the dominoes toppling requires some practice to master. Dominoes are fast! As a tip, we recommend following the action with the camera zoomed out a little bit and zooming in within editing software later for better and easier tracking. If you are going to carry a camera, it helps to have one with good image stabilization. These setups tend to be built all at once for seamless action.

Total Capture Videos

These videos capture the entire setup from beginning to end but the camera angle and position doesn't move. These videos usually require larger setups to have any length to them. Keep in mind though the larger the run the wider the camera angle has to be and the smaller the dominoes will look in the video. An easy way to add time to this style of video is to get the run toppling with multiple cameras and angles. Then show each camera angle in succession in the video, letting viewers watch the same run fall multiple times and from different angles. Dominoes fall so fast it takes a second or two to take it all in.

Slow Motion Videos

These videos require a good slow motion capable camera. It is important that you don't bore your viewers with shots that are disinteresting in slow motion. So, picking specific, epic moments to slow down in the video is usually appropriate. Dominoes fall fast and their reactions look really neat in slow motion. These setups can be very short with some high action event in it, because the slow motion effects draw the video's time length out to be much longer.

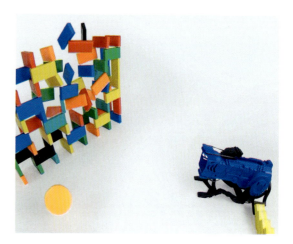

There are plenty of platforms to share your videos online: YouTube, Instagram, Facebook, and more! We look forward to seeing them online.

Be sure your camera has a memory card in it.

setting Domino Records

Join the Bulk Dominoes Leaderboards! This is the place to go for fun domino competition, challenges, and to show off talents. There are plenty of categories to explore and setting records is a cinch. Once a record seems interesting enough, just go for it! Use Pro, Mini, Mini-Micro dominoes, or Kinetic Planks to set a record. If you're up for the challenge, become the Bulk Dominoes Grand Champion by having the most individual number 1 records from our categories to reign supreme.

Combine your efforts and set records by working as a group. A lot of activities are simply more fun as a team and toppling dominoes is no exception. Each category has group records available. So invite some friends over, choose a category to conquer, video the whole attempt, and submit it. You can find all the rules and guidelines online at bulkdominoes.com.

Single Chain • Spirals • Walls • Height • 2D Pyramid • 3D Pyramid
Cube • Fall Wall • Lightning Run • Fields • Lightning Field • Stack
Speedy Setup • Toppled Per Minute • Longest Run Time • Underwater
Bridges • Spinners • Rapid Track • Most Cups

Domino Clubs

Dominoes are fun and entertaining to play with and watch, so why not join or make a domino club? Domino clubs are starting all over the world! Start with after school programs, college clubs, religious activities, library and museums events, online groups, friends, and family gatherings. So, what are you waiting for? Get together and start sharing your passion for stacking and building domino chain reactions!

SCIENCE | TECHNOLOGY | ENGINEERING | ARTS | MATHEMATICS

Domino FUN!

There are other uses for dominoes. They can be used for a variety of games. These games listed here are similar to some of the games that we played growing up and are a lot of fun. Playing these games can really inspire domino topplers to get imaginative, have a great time, and even create games of their own.

GAMES

Domino Wars - players start with the same number of dominoes on each side of the room. They use them to build a structure and defensive walls. The minimum structure to defend must have 2 walls and a roof. Once setup is complete the game begins and players use the domino launcher to launch ping pong balls at each other's buildings to try to knock down the main defensive structure. If it falls and the minimum requirement of 2 walls and a roof is not met, the other player is the victor. This can be played with multiple people, just try not to get caught in the crossfire. No player can block anything with hands or body, it's all up to your defenses.

Destroy that CITY! Two or more people take the dominoes they have and build up a city of structures. Once the city has been built each player places their "pawn" somewhere in the city. Then each player takes turns launching ping pong balls with the domino launcher trying to knock down the other player's pawns. The last player with their pawn still standing wins. It helps if there is a designated launching area that players have to launch behind/in.

CHALLENGES

Minute Challenge - This is a competition to see how many dominoes can be set up in a minute and then topple them all down with a single starting point. The dominoes all have to topple in order to count.

20 Domino Building Challenge - See how many different towers you can make with 20 dominoes. Take pictures of each one. What is the hardest structure that can be made with only 20 dominoes? This is a great game for teachers in classroom settings.

Ceiling Challenge - First one to build their tower of dominoes to the ceiling wins!

Trick Sequence Challenge - Make a list of your favorite tricks. Cut them out, and draw five out of a hat. Make a setup using the drawn tricks from the hat, performed in the order they were pulled. If they all connect and topple successfully, you win!

Index

Basic Line	16
Basic Split	17
Diamond Split	17
Domino Bridges	19
Domino Stairs	19
Flow Spiral	16
Leaning Turn	18
Lightning Run	19
Multi Split	17
Safety Gap	17
Segments	19
Simple Curve	16
Spiral	16
Tight Turn	18
Turn	18

Basic Crossover	22
Click Clacks	32
Cluster	34
Coaster Rail	39
Cobra Coils	35
Colonnade	32
Color Flipper	28
Column Crossover	39
Column Drop	38
Double Synchronizer	25
Forked Lightning	36
High Hurdles	38
Jitter Hitter	25
Lateral Crossover	29
Lateral Wave	36
Lightning Bolt	30
Lightning Circuit	31
Lightning Storm	30
Line Chopper	31
Little Nudge	32
Loop + Swoop	29
Missing Link	27
Pagoda Crossover	35

Pergola	32
Piston Switch	23
Pi Towers	33
Resonator	41
Reverse V- Booster	40
Reverters	36
Rickrack	37
Running The Gauntlet	41
Secure Crossover	22
Sheet Lightning	33
Snake Run	33
Space Ships	40
Sparks	34
Speed Crossover	23
Springboard Corner	34
Stanchion	35
Superbolt	38
Surfboard Switch	38
The Chute	24
The Comeback	26
The Jitter	25
The Reverse	24
The Sea Serpent	34
The Synchronizer	25
The Zipper	37
V- Booster	40

Basic Field	44
Chain Lightning Field Starter	47
Circle Field	45
Cross Fields	48
Diagonal Field	49
Flag Pole Field Starter	45
Horizontal Field	44
Lightning Field	49
Mid-Field Crossover	48
Power Dive Field Starter	47
Reciprocating Field	46

Alternator	62
Cannon Ball	59
Dragon's Teeth	62
Fainting Face Plant	55
Hand Spring	54
Horizontal Flips	57
Hurdle Kicks	64
Instant Transfer	61
Power Dive	65
Quantum Jump	61
Reciprocator	59
Roundhouse Kick	60
Sailor's Dive	65
Sleepers	63
Stacked Launcher	63
Steam Roller	58
The Cleaver	t56
The Double Stun	60
The Hammer	57
The Stun	60
Vertical Lightning	56
Vertigo	56
Wave Rider	64

Basic Tower	83
Battering Ram	104
Castle	92
Criss Cross Fall Wall	84
Double Take	83
Fall Wall	84
Horizontal Wall	82
Imploding Tower	96
Knockout Tower	102
Lighting Pyramid	85
Lightning Tower	99
Lightning Weave	85
Pagoda Pyramid	87
Pyramid	89
Pyramid Wall	88
Razor Back Pyramid	92
Speed Pyramid	86
Speed Wall Pyramid	86
Spiral Speed Wall	100
The Cube	95
The Stack	104
The Waterfall	94
Tower Siege	94
Tower Tumble	94
Wall	86
Wall Splitter	90

Bermuda Triangle	68
Bolstered Bermuda Triangle	69
Cascading Wave	72
Dino Bones	74
Double Kilter Run	78
Double Reverse Wave	76
Dragon Dance	77
Fireworks	71
Herringbone	75
Kilter Run	78
Pizza Slices	79
Reverse Wave	76
Ripple Wave	77
Running Tall	76
Simultaneous Drop	79
Splitting Bolts	73
Stalactite	78
The Caterpillar	73
The Gravitator	74
Trellis Wave	77
Zipper Pull	70

180°	108
180° Hand-Off Maintained	108
180° Maintained	108
All In	109
Bridges With 4-Way Splitter	110
Bridge With Straight Track	110
Extended Hand-Off	109
Flipping Arcs	111
Graduated Blocks	117
Half Spin	109
Lock "N" Load	115
Potentials	116
Rack 'em Up	113
Ripcord	114
Rolling Arcs	111
Round About	109
Single Bridge	110
The Double	112
The Single	112
Top "N" Drop	114

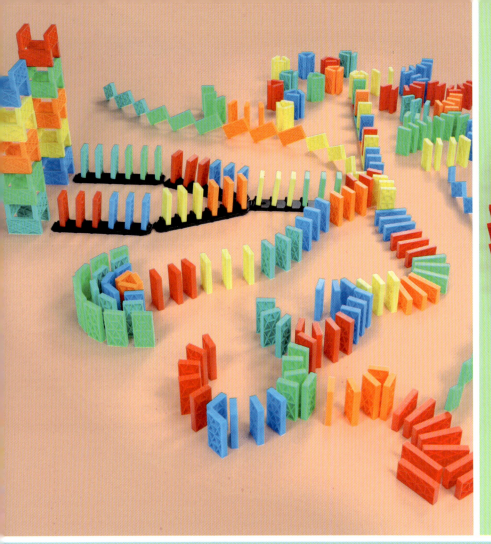
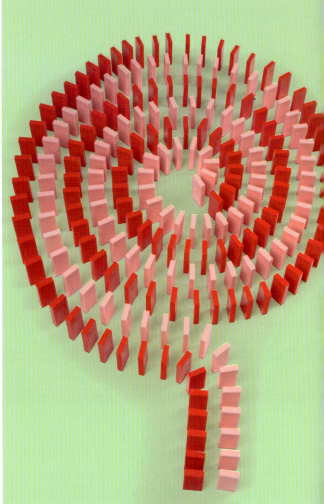

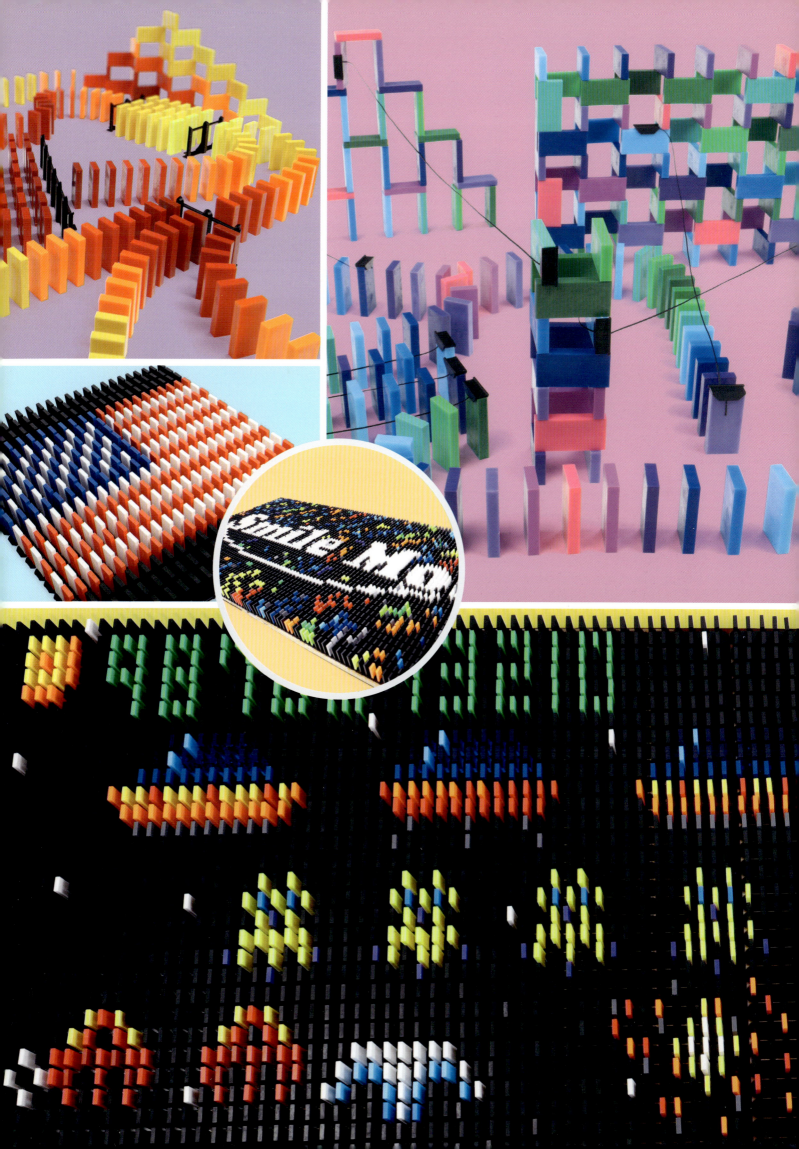

Join the Bulk Dominoes Family

BULKDOMINOES.COM

At Bulk Dominoes, we are constantly innovating and creating fun, new, S.T.E.A.M. oriented products for a variety of ages. We offer a fun unique way to engage critical thinking, strategy, creativity, and problem solving. Get involved with Bulk Dominoes and become a brand ambassador! We are always looking for talented domino builders to push the limits of creativity.

Sign up for our email list for exclusive offers and specials on all our latest products.

JOIN US ON SOCIAL

Join us on social for fun daily content, inspiration, and the latest in domino excitement!

 Bulkdominoes   **@bulkdominoes**

 @BulkDominoes   **Bulk Dominoes**